THE JOHN HARVARD LIBRARY

Bernard Bailyn
Editor-in-Chief

THE JOHN HARVARD LIBRARY

DEMOCRACY AND SOCIAL ETHICS

By

JANE ADDAMS

Edited by Anne Firor Scott

THE BELKNAP PRESS OF

HARVARD UNIVERSITY PRESS

Cambridge, Massachusetts

CONTENTS

INTRODUCTION

The events of the years from the Civil War to the First World War were dominated by the rapid emergence of an urban-industrial society. The nature of this change was far from clear to the participants. Nothing like this had happened before in the United States, and the earlier development in England was only partly understood and assimilated. Inevitably, certain thoughtful people tried to make sense of it. Jane Addams was one of these, and *Democracy and Social Ethics* one of the most interesting efforts to achieve an intellectual grasp of what was happening. Its thesis was the thesis of her life: that the time had come to add a social ethic to democracy.

i

To be born in Illinois in 1860 was to bridge two eras. The life of Jane Addams' father, John Huy Addams, symbolized the earlier one. Serving as a miller's apprentice in Pennsylvania, he married his employer's daughter and set out, in 1844, for frontier Illinois. After examining a number of prospects he chose a spot six miles from Freeport, where he bought a sawmill and a gristmill on a small stream dignified with the name of Cedar River and began to make his way in the world, first as a miller and later as a banker. John Addams was clearly a builder rather than a speculator. For sixteen years a member of the Illinois legislature, he worked for internal improvements which would speed the economic development of the state. In due course he became the leading citizen of Stephenson County. Four of his eight children grew to maturity; of these Jane Addams, born September 6, 1860, was the youngest.

Her father's life stood for the great days of the frontier; her own for the urban age. Her early childhood caught echoes of the great debate over slavery, in which her father's friend Abraham Lincoln was a key figure. "It is curious," she wrote years later, "how children catch the glow of moral enthusiasm of their elders and absorb opinions by listening." [1]

Upon the death of her mother when she was two, the little girl fixed her affection upon her father. It is impossible now to disentangle the real John Addams from her image of him as a

[1] Jane Addams, *My Friend Julia Lathrop* (New York, 1935), p. 25.

being wise and great, of immense personal rectitude, guided by an "inner light." She loved to tell the story of Lincoln's letter to her father written when both were in the Illinois legislature, addressed to "My dear double-D'd Addams" and saying that he knew well that Mr. Addams would vote as his conscience dictated but that it would be a help to know which way that conscience was pointing! "Doubtless I centered upon him," Jane Addams wrote, "all the careful imitation which a little girl ordinarily gives to her mother's ways and habits. My mother had died when I was a baby and my father's second marriage did not occur until my eighth year." [2]

At an age when little girls were commonly expected to model themselves upon housewifely mothers, she was emulating an effective and active father, who had a strong sense of social responsibility. A curious aspect of this relationship was that Jane Addams was convinced that she was herself an ugly duckling. Early pictures show an engaging child, but her own self-image was shaped by a "crooked back"—a spinal defect

[2] Jane Addams, *Twenty Years at Hull-House* (New York, 1910), p. 11. This book is a sensitive retrospective analysis of her first fifty years, and is indispensable for any one interested in her thought.

which made her carry her head slightly to one side. She worried that such a homely child might disgrace her handsome father.

Anna Haldeman, John Addams' second wife, was an energetic woman who knew books and music and shared her knowledge with the Addams children. There were two Haldeman sons. One became Jane's constant playmate; the other later married her sister Alice.

Jane Addams looked back upon her childhood as a time of physical freedom and liberty of the imagination, a wide-ranging outdoor life lived largely in the company of her stepbrother, George Haldeman. After the manner of Victorian fathers, John Addams rewarded her for every "life" from Plutarch read and reported, and paid as well for every volume she read of such things as Irving's *Life of Washington*. Although nearby Freeport seemed a true city in contrast to Cedarville, there was little to make her aware of the great industrial society which was coming into being in Chicago and New York. What echoes she caught of this larger and more complex world came from books, or from grown-up conversation.

She was aware of the world beyond Cedarville, and at seventeen wanted badly to go to Smith

College, then recently opened to provide an education for women equal to any available to men. Her father had other plans. Jane was to go to Rockford Female Seminary, as her sisters had, and be "finished off" afterward with a European tour. John Addams' view prevailed and in 1877 she went off somewhat rebelliously to Rockford.

Life at the seminary was simple and rigorous. Each girl took care of her own room and built her own fire. The intellectual and moral atmosphere was permeated with religious fervor, reflecting the spiritual climate of the Victorian era and the intense idealism of these early college women. The curriculum encompassed Latin, Greek, natural science, ancient history and literature, mental and moral philosophy, and French. The high point of the week for Jane Addams was Sunday morning which she customarily spent reading the Greek testament with a favorite teacher.

From the fragmentary record of her Rockford years it is possible to catch a hint of a developing personality of more than ordinary force. This slight, shy, provincial girl not only showed signs of being unusually able but also of having unusual personal magnetism. In some mysterious way she became the center of her class—a fact

which was reflected in the reactions to her of both
teachers and fellow students. She was dissatisfied
with the intellectual range of the curriculum and
joined a group of students and teachers who read
together Shakespeare, George Eliot, Carlyle,
Browning and Ruskin. From her letters it appears that Carlyle and Ruskin particularly influenced her early efforts to think about herself
and her relation to the world.

I, for my part, am convinced that the success of that
work [one's calling] depends upon our religion and
that I can never go ahead and use my best powers until I do settle it. It seems to me sometimes—I suppose
when I am wrought up—could I but determine *that*
and have it for a sure basis, that with time and space
to work in I could train my powers to anything, it
would only remain to choose what. Of course this may
be a false stress laid on religion but I don't fuss any-
more, since I have discovered its importance but go
ahead building up my religion wherever I can find it,
from the Bible and observation, from books and people
and in no small degree from Carlyle.[3]

Two months later she struck the same note again:

I only feel that I need religion in a practical sense, that

[3] Jane Addams to Ellen Gates Starr, Nov. 22, 1879, Sophia Smith
Collection, Smith College, Northampton, Mass. Cf. Thomas Carlyle,
Sartor Resartus (London, 1838), pp. 169–170. All letters cited from
Jane Addams to Ellen Starr are in this collection.

if I could fix my relations to God & the universe, & so be in perfect harmony with nature & deity, I could use my faculties and energy so much better and could do almost anything.[4]

At the same time she was plagued by self-doubt. She tried the experiment of not praying for three months and felt none the worse for it. Though there was no touch of arrogance in her letters, there were hints that she occasionally felt that she saw more deeply than other people. Her search for a religious meaning for life was complicated by the fundamentalist atmosphere of Rockford, with which she was not in sympathy, and by the pressure—which she steadfastly resisted—to become a missionary. As a rebel against the prevailing fundamentalism she was forced to define her own religious position. Her inclination was toward some universal religion, some Primal Cause, of which Christianity was only one manifestation.

At Rockford the hallmark of her adult mind was already beginning to appear: the combination of a mystical-intuitive turn of mind with a down-to-earth interest in how things worked and a fine capacity for observation. Intellectual curiosity she had in good measure, as her wide reading and

[4] Jane Addams to Ellen Starr, Jan. 29, 1889.

interest in scientific experiments demonstrated. Spiritual curiosity she had too, and introspection accompanied observation. In her textbooks she encountered Darwin whose mark upon her later thinking would be considerable.

If the underlying motif of her college career was one of constant searching for spiritual answers, the surface was one of achievement. She was valedictorian in 1881 and had a hand in almost every student activity. Plans for her own future were vague; she still thought of going to Smith, but at other times she wrote of a desire to go to Edinburgh and study medicine. The summer of 1881, like summers before it, was given over to visiting and being visited, to much reading and discussion of books. In August a great blow fell. Her beloved father, at 59, died of a ruptured appendix. All hopes, plans, ambitions, fell in a heap. She wrote her closest friend:

I will not write of myself or how purposeless and without ambition I am, only prepare yourself so you won't be too disappointed in me when you come. The greatest sorrow that can ever come to me has past and I hope it is only a question of time until I get my moral purposes straightened.[5]

Her search for direction and purpose had been

[5] Jane Addams to Ellen Starr, Sept. 3, 1881.

INTRODUCTION

guided by the image of her father; now that he
was gone all was confusion. His death brought,
she said, "realization of sorrow as the common lot,
of death as the universal experience."

Idleness did not help; in the late fall she enrolled at the Woman's Medical College in Phila-
delphia. Before she was well launched there, the
old spinal ailment flared up and she left the
classroom for the hospital. In September 1882
her stepbrother and now brother-in-law, Harry
Haldeman, a surgeon, thought he had a solution.
An operation ensued, followed by a long con-
valescence. In January 1883 she spoke of the "las-
situde, melancholy and general crookedness"
which beset her, but added that she was "emerging with a straight back and a fresh hold on life
and endeavor, I hope." [6]

Before the "fresh hold" could become very
strong her older brother James Weber Addams
developed a mental illness, and she felt obliged to
help out with his affairs. To her surprise she
found herself adept at business, and wondered if
she was about to lose "all hold of the softer graces
and refinements." [7] When Weber improved
enough to come home from the hospital, Jane

[6] Jane Addams to Ellen Starr, Jan. 7, 1883.
[7] Jane Addams to Ellen Starr, April 24, 1883.

Addams and her stepmother sailed for Europe. The purpose was the deferred "finishing" which her father had planned, and perhaps also an effort to shake clear of the melancholy which had dogged her for two years. The prospect was exciting but she was not altogether happy. Was one really justified in seeking culture and personal pleasure in a world so full of trouble? Once in Europe, she studied art and languages with unusual diligence. She was also very much aware of the life around her: of the inhabitants of London's East End buying decayed vegetables at auction; of the bowed German women carrying heavy loads of hot beer from the brewery to the cooling room. She had a natural affinity for the places where there was want and oppression and yet the more she saw of such things the more the feeling of futility and misplaced energy in her own life increased.

In Italy she was moved by religious painting and the lives of early Christians depicted in the catacombs. The image of the saintly life which had intrigued her years before renewed its fascination:

The grand series of frescoes which carry on a sainted life from one event to another with increasing enthusiasm, until the very apotheosis when they are lost in a cloud of angelic heads never fail to affect me with a tremor and a corresponding desire for the power arising from mere goodness.[8]

The search for a purpose for life went on. Back in the United States, her malaise seemed no better:

I am always floundering when I deal with religious nomenclature or sensations simply because my religious life has been so small;—for many years it was my ambition to reach my father's moral requirements and now when I am needing something more, I find myself approaching a crisis—& looking wistfully to my friends for help.[9]

She suffered from a paralysis of will. When her stepmother decided to go to Baltimore where George Haldeman was studying at Johns Hopkins, Jane dutifully went along, though "filled with shame that with all my apparent leisure I do nothing." [10]

When summer came she visited her married sisters and then returned to Cedarville. Nowhere could she find peace. During one of these summers she was baptized, not because of any sudden

[8] Jane Addams to Ellen Starr, March 9, 1884.
[9] Jane Addams to Ellen Starr, Dec. 6, 1885.
[10] Jane Addams to Ellen Starr, Feb. 7, 1886.

conversion but because she had concluded that it was conceit to think of "being good in one's own right." [11] Finally, in the fall of 1887, in company with her closest friend, Ellen Gates Starr, and her former teacher, Sarah Anderson, she embarked again for Europe. Her own self-assessments were harsh at this point. Ellen Starr saw something different, and in a letter from Rome reported:

Jane devoted most of her time at table to an absurd old Missourian who wore a flannel shirt and a paper collar, speared his bread with his fork . . . and picked his teeth at the table, and whom nobody else near him would take the trouble to talk to. I never admired her more. She talked to this man as she would have done to a man of the world. I don't know what I would not give to have what prompts her and makes it possible for her to act this way. I suppose what I would not give is the moral effort and self discipline which is required to develop a character like hers. It seems more beautiful to me as I know it better, and would be worth more to me than all Europe if I could become only a little like her. All of which would fairly shrivel her if she could see it and I feel as if I had in some way been unfair to her to write it.[12]

[11] *Twenty Years at Hull-House*, p. 78.
[12] Ellen Gates Starr to Mrs. John H. Addams, Jan. 30 and Feb. 5, 1888. Sophia Smith Collection.

Though their journey was superficially the usual pursuit of art and culture, for Jane Addams it was still a search for the answer to the fundamental question: What is good? Upon this would depend what she was to do with her life.

In the spring of 1888 a revelation came. She was in Madrid, and with her friends went to a bullfight. Long after the others had left "in faintness and disgust" she had continued to watch, caught up, she said, "in the vivid association of an historical survival" and not thinking much about the bloodshed. In the evening came a reaction; she was ashamed to have been so carried away by the pageantry as to have been made unaware of suffering, and in a moment of moral revulsion found herself re-examining her whole way of life. It suddenly seemed that dreams of future greatness had been allowed to substitute for present effort, that she had fallen into "the meanest type of self-deception." In this mood she crystallized a plan that had long been forming in her mind: she would go to a large city, find a house in the middle of the poorest district, and begin to live as a neighbor to the very poor.

William James once described religious conversion as the process "by which a self hitherto

divided, consciously wrong, inferior and unhappy, becomes unified and consciously superior
and happy ..." [13] After this experience in Madrid
Jane Addams was not a different person, but her
seeking, searching, and self-doubt gave way to
purpose, drive, conviction, and inner poise. This
communicated itself to other people. Ellen Starr
wrote in the year Hull-House opened:

She strengthens the weak knees and supports the feeble
hands, and has no sense of strength herself. It is a
strange and beautiful thing for me to see. Everybody who
comes near her is affected by her. It is as if she simply
diffused something which comes from outside herself
of which she is the luminous medium.[14]

Jane Addams' own forecast of ten years earlier,
"if I could fix my relations to God and the universe, & so be in perfect harmony with nature &
deity, I could do almost anything," was on the
verge of fulfillment. In four years this doubtful
girl known only to her family and friends would
become a national figure and be on her way to
becoming one of the most famous Americans of
her day.

[13] William James, *The Varieties of Religious Experience* (New
York, 1961).
[14] Ellen Gates Starr to Mary Allen, Sept. 15, 1889, Sophia Smith
Collection.

The particular path she chose was the result of the confluence of many forces. Jane Addams' early reading in Carlyle and Ruskin had laid the foundation. In the 1880's she was assimilating the *Fabian Essays,* and Charles Booth's *Life and Labor of the People of London.* Positivism, to which she had been introduced by Comte's English disciple Frederic Harrison, appealed to her and for a while she had thought Comte's religion of humanity might be the answer to her long quest for a doctrine sufficiently broad to encompass real life. Echoes of Comte would appear in her writing for years.

Jane Addams' first encounter with Tolstoy may have come at about this time. Toward the end of her life she wrote that his *What To Do Then* had profoundly modified her religious convictions, and commented that its power had been greater because of the "widespread moral malaise in regard to existing social conditions," which existed in the late eighties. Her description of the influence of Tolstoy may be read in the light of the decision she took in Spain: "The doctrine must be understood through the deed. It is the only possible way not only to stir others into action but to give the message itself a sense of reality. 'Certain virtues are formed in man by his doing the action,' said Aristotle." [15]

The specific notion of a house among the poor had been part of her earlier plan of studying medicine, and owed something also to the experiments of English college men reaching back to the late 1860's, most strikingly embodied in Toynbee Hall, which she had visited once. She was beginning to formulate what would become one of her central ideas, that of conduct as a means of propaganda. [16] She was much moved by the idea of universal brotherhood, an idea which was also central to Tolstoy's thought.

Once the decision was reached, action seemed easy. Ellen Starr agreed to join the plan. Thereupon Jane left for London, to learn as much as

[15] Jane Addams, "A Book That Changed My Life," *Christian Century*, 44:1196–1198 (Oct. 13, 1927). Cf. Carlyle: "But indeed Conviction, were it never so excellent, is worthless till it converts itself into Conduct. Nay properly Conviction is not possible till then; inasmuch as all Speculation is by nature endless, formless, a vortex amid vortices: only by a felt indubitable certainty of Experience, does it find any centre to revolve around, and so fashion itself into a system. Most true it is, as a wise man teaches us, that Doubt of any sort cannot be removed except by Action." Thomas Carlyle, *Sartor Resartus* (London, 1838), p. 201.

[16] See Jane Addams, "Tolstoy and Gandhi," *Christian Century*, 48:1485–1488 (Nov. 25, 1931), for one of many statements of this idea. Until she went to Chicago in 1889 the chief intellectual influences seem to have been English and European rather than American.

she could from Samuel and Henrietta Barnett at Toynbee Hall, thinking this the best preparation available to her. "We realised that she was a great soul and took pains to show her much and tell her more," Mrs. Barnett wrote years later.[17]

The ideas of Canon Barnett, and of his mentor, Octavia Hill, were influential, but from the beginning it was clear that the basis of this enterprise would be Jane Addams' own convictions. She and Ellen Starr went to Chicago to look for an appropriate location and for people who might help. Miss Starr explained their guiding ideas in a letter to her sister:

After we have been there long enough & people see that we don't catch diseases, & that vicious people do not destroy us or our property, we think we have well-founded reason to believe that there are at least half a dozen girls in the city who will be glad to come & stay for awhile & learn to know the people & understand them and their ways of life: to give them what they have out of their culture and leisure & overindulgence, & to receive the culture which comes of self-denial, poverty & failure, which these people have always known. There is to be no "organization" & no "institution" about it. The world is overstocked with institutions

---

[17] Henrietta Barnett, *Canon Barnett: His Life, Work and Friends* (London, 1921), p. 422. Jane Addams' relationship with the Barnetts lasted as long as they lived.

and organizations; & after all, a personality is the only
thing that ever touches anybody.

. . . . .

Jane's idea which she puts very much to the front and on
no account will give up is that it is more for the benefit
of the people who do it than for the other class . . .
The truth is, the thing is in the air. People are coming
to the conclusion that if anything is to be done towards
tearing down these walls—half imaginary between
classes, that are making anarchists and strikers the
order of the day it must be done by actual contact and
done voluntarily from the top.[18]

That there was trouble in the air in Chicago
and other large cities by 1889 there could be no
doubt. Three years had passed since the Haymarket bombing with its electric effect upon
people's thinking about "the social question."
Half a century later Jane Addams wrote of "the
startling reaction to the Haymarket riot . . . which
introduced dynamite into the social conflict and
so terrified the entire region that it exhibited
symptoms of shell shock for decades afterward." [19]

There was bitterness unlike anything yet seen
in America. Henry George had suggested it in

[18] Ellen Gates Starr to Mary Blaisdell, Feb. 23, 1889, Sophia
Smith Collection.
[19] *My Friend Julia Lathrop*, p. 46.

Progress and Poverty in 1879; it was evident in William Dean Howells' steady progression toward socialism; it would appear in the literature of criticism coming or soon to come from Hamlin Garland, Theodore Dreiser, Frank Norris. Foreign-born intellectuals such as Emma Goldman and Alexander Berkman tried to lead their fellow immigrants into drastic solutions. In Chicago and New York anarchists, socialists, communists agreed on one principle—the need for revolutionary change.

In Chicago where nearly eighty per cent of the people were immigrants or children of immigrants, it was perfectly possible for the well-to-do natives to live their whole lives without first-hand contact with the vast population which did the hard, dirty work in the stockyards, on the streets, in the garment trade, work which was making a handful of capitalists very rich, work which accounted for the extraordinarily rapid growth of Chicago in the decades after the Civil War. The immigrants were equally isolated, in their desperate efforts to make a new life in a world which had turned out to be so different from the dreamed-of promised land. The situation was more explosive because of the image of the United

States as a place where no man who was willing to work need go hungry. The 1880's and 1890's saw a violence of protest which hitherto had seemed appropriate only to a European despotism.

In choosing to go to live in an immigrant district Jane Addams was taking a practical step, but the main issue was, she felt, a moral one, and the attack on it would come, in her own words, as the result of a "certain Renaissance in Christianity." People's ideas, and ethical values, would have to develop to meet the changing situation. It was no longer sufficient to feel responsible for the well-being of one's own family, friends, and social equals. A new social ethic would have to evolve which would be based on responsibility to the whole community. This is essence was the purpose of Hull-House, and it was to this end that she turned her capacities as a leader, and teacher in the broadest sense of the word.

The house itself was found after a long search. It had been built as a country home for a wealthy Chicago real estate man and—symbolic of the rapid growth of the city—in thirty-odd years had become totally surrounded by an immense, closely packed immigrant colony: the nineteenth ward.

When Charles Hull's heir gave Jane Addams and Ellen Starr a four-year lease, rent free, the name of the builder was adopted in gratitude.

For a decade both Hull-House and its founder grew remarkably—the house in physical size and variety of function, Jane Addams in purpose and ideas, in depth and breadth of social understanding, and in satisfaction with life. Twelve years later, recovering from a train accident, she could write, "I find this morning, the first downstairs, filled with a content so deep that it reminds me of the early days of H-H." [20]

Other people came to join the venture and to stimulate Jane Addams' development. Julia Lathrop, who eventually became a member of the Illinois State Board of Charities and head of the Federal Children's Bureau, had known Jane Addams at Rockford and had gone on to study at Vassar. A prolific innovator in the new field of social work, she was a wise as well as a witty woman, and was greatly valued by all the residents of Hull-House, with which she was associated for forty-one years (1889-1932). One of

[20] Jane Addams to Mary Rozet Smith, May 19, 1902, Jane Addams Papers, Swarthmore College Peace Collection.

INTRODUCTION

Jane Addams' last writings was the biography *My Friend Julia Lathrop*, a book that does much to illuminate both their lives.

Florence Kelley had a different style, but she was also a strong and effective woman, with whom life was always interesting and seldom peaceful. Daughter of Congressman William D. ("Pig-Iron") Kelley, she had gone to Corneli when it was first opened to women, studied in Europe, translated Engels, married a European doctor and borne three children before she appeared at Hull-House in 1893 looking for a base of operations from which to support her children, after the failure of her marriage. The most hard-driving of the group, she had a large hand in drafting the first Illinois Factory Law and was appointed Factory Inspector by Governor Altgeld. When a change of political control led to her dismissal, and the courts annulled the law, she went on to New York and built the Consumers League into an effective tool for improving working conditions. She described her work in a book called *Some Ethical Gains Through Legislation*.

Alice Hamilton was younger than the others, and came to Hull-House after she heard Jane Addams speak on its work. Trained in medicine, she turned her knowledge to social account in an effort to secure safety regulation in the "dangerous trades." She virtually invented the field of industrial medicine, a fact the Harvard Medical School would ultimately recognize by making her its first woman faculty member.[21]

The history of Hull-House was related to many significant historical developments. Not least of these was its effect upon the rapidly changing role of women in American life. In addition to the central group of Jane Addams, Julia Lathrop, Florence Kelley and Alice Hamilton, each of whom was destined to work on the national and international stage, numbers of other women used Hull-House as a base from which to develop significant professional or volunteer careers. Among the best known, Mary Smith, Mary Wilmarth, Louise DeKoven Bowen, and Ellen Starr were Jane Addams' contemporaries, volunteers who helped develop the characteristic Hull-House programs and financed its causes. Later, Grace and Edith Abbott and Sophinisba Breckinridge combined service at Hull-House with scholarly and professional careers; they all taught at the

[21] Alice Hamilton, *Exploring the Dangerous Trades* (New York, 1944).

University of Chicago School of Civics and Philanthropy, and both Edith Abbott and Sophinisba Breckinridge became deans of the school. Grace Abbott headed the Immigrants Protective League, succeeded Julia Lathrop as head of the U.S. Children's Bureau and ultimately represented the United States in the International Labor Organization.

Jane Addams through her life thought much about the role of women. From her early days at Rockford she aimed toward independence for herself, and she worked in many ways to achieve a new relationship between the sexes in American society. She also spoke frequently of woman's historic role and of the home as the original center of civilization. Much of her social effort was directed toward securing for other women the right to stay at home and care for their children, rather than being forced into the labor market. She wanted to preserve what was good in the traditional role and at the same time help society to formulate a new view which would accept a wider range of possible life styles for women. Her own example and the encouragement that the Hull-House group offered, did a great deal to socialize woman's role and to bring the power of women to bear upon public problems.

The road by which she came to these convictions and to her own life pattern is only partly clear. The six years of freedom in her early life before a stepmother came on the scene may have spoiled her for the deference to men commonly expected of married women in her day. Her admiration for her father and her efforts to imitate him at a formative period shaped her in a different mold from the one traditional for girls. Rockford itself, a pioneering effort for women's education, had provided an atmosphere in which students felt, Jane Addams said, "that each moment of time thus dearly bought must be conscientiously used."

In her surviving correspondence there are only a few references to romance, but there is evidence that she was sought after by several young men, and fifteen years after Hull-House opened she still spoke of love leading to marriage as the "highest gift which life can offer to a woman." Toward the end of her life she explained the fact that she and so many of her friends had remained single:

For a considerable period after the door of opportunity began to be slowly opened to woman, she was practically faced with an alternative of marriage or a career. She could not have both apparently for two reasons. Men did not at first want to marry women of the new type, and women could not fulfill the two functions of profession and homemaking until modern invention had made a new type of housekeeping practicable, and perhaps one should add, until public opinion tolerated the double role.[22]

A post-Freudian age will surely ask "Is this all?" Did her early attachment to the image of a father cast in heroic mold eliminate most of the young men who showed signs of romantic interest? In her sixth decade (by that time a post-Freudian herself) she speculated about the group of women who had been "selected by pioneer qualities of character and sometimes at least by the divine urge of intellectual hunger . . ." Had they, in choosing to be self-supporting and devoting themselves to public affairs, missed the central meaning of woman's life? She consulted her friend Emily Greene Balch, chairman of Wellesley's economics department, who was thinking of the same question. Miss Balch wrote:

Is it compatible with the modern theories about sex that two generations of professionally trained women lived, without vows or outward safeguards, completely celibate lives with no sense of its being difficult or of

[22] Jane Addams, *The Second Twenty Years at Hull-House* (New York, 1930), p. 196.

being misunderstood? Some of them later married; most of them did not. Now they are old or oldish women, how do they feel about it?

She went on to say that they were willing to admit that they had suffered a serious loss, but not at all willing to admit that they were abnormal.

If the educated unmarried woman of the period between the Civil War and the World War represent an unique phase, it is one that has important implications which have not yet been adequately recognized by those who insist upon the imperious claims of sex.[23]

Jane Addams had written elsewhere that as ". . . that modern relationship between men and women, which the Romans called 'virtue between equals' increases, [it] will continue to make women freer and nobler, less timid of reputation and more human." [24] She herself met men on equal terms, and developed close and lasting friendships with a wide range of them. John Dewey, William James, Graham Taylor, Henry Demarest Lloyd, William Kent, Robert Morss Lovett were only a few who gave her not only respect but admiration and affection.

Yet her own closest affection was reserved for

[23] *The Second Twenty Years,* pp. 197–198.
[24] *A New Conscience and an Ancient Evil* (New York, 1911), p. 212.

women and children. It was to Ellen Starr, for example, that she unburdened herself in college, and at the time Hull-House began they showed a marked dependence upon each other. "I need you, dear one, more than you can realize." "A day without a letter is *blanc,* as the French say of a sleepless night. I don't like such a day at all," were typical comments in her letters to Miss Starr.

Mary Rozet Smith, daughter of a wealthy Chicago family, came to Hull-House in its first year and though she never became a regular resident, was as much a part of its life as if she had been. Younger than Jane Addams, beautiful, and endowed with an extraordinarily warm and generous spirit, she became, in time, in Jane Addams' words "the person I love best." The depth of this affection and the manner of its expression in a long series of letters, many sent only from one side of Chicago to another, are essential to an understanding of Jane Addams. They strike a note of dependency, as well as of intellectual comradeship. Mary Smith and her family were large contributors to Hull-House, and since Jane Addams spent her own income for the House it was Mary Smith who supplied the new dress, the trip to Europe and—later—the summer cottage; such amenities as Jane Addams' busy life left time for.

Close ties bound the whole Hull-House group. Julia Lathrop, Florence Kelley, Alice Hamilton and Louise DeKoven Bowen were all attracted to Hull-House by Jane Addams, and all went on to far-reaching achievement in their own right. Strong personalities all, it would have been strange if they had always agreed, and in fact their lively discussions were high points in the life of Hull-House. They reinforced each other in a day when independent women were still the exception, and developed a strong sense of responsibility for their mutual well-being. The friendship between them was broken only by death.

The first years were exciting. They were also difficult years when it often seemed that the pattern was one step forward, two steps back. In retrospect these years would be seen as misted over with fatigue. There was so much to do, and the means were relatively so small, that there never seemed time to rest. The great industrial depression of 1893 brought home the problem of urban unemployment with full force, and led Jane Addams to her first serious reading in economics. She became deeply involved in the

INTRODUCTION

Chicago Civic Federation and in an effort to
mediate the Pullman strike in 1894. The Pullman
affair added to the existing unrest and unemployment, and the experience bit deep into Jane
Adams' consciousness.

The population of the nineteenth ward was
almost totally immigrant: Russian, Italian, Irish,
German, and miscellaneous other nationalities.
Jane Addams' sensitive observations in many of
their native lands prepared her to be almost the
first articulate American to understand the feelings of these people, newly uprooted from ancient
cultures and thrown willy-nilly into the maw
of an American city. She was concerned for the
loss of skills and cultural traditions of the home-
land, the confusion in family life, the physical
and political exploitation which overcame them.
Much of her time and thought was devoted to
them.

In the context of the immigrant neighborhood
Hull-House set out to find solutions to the problems of a fast-growing city. The residents were
prolific social innovators. The first juvenile
court in the world grew out of the daily experience of Hull-House with delinquents, and later
this same court pioneered in the application of
psychiatric treatment of youthful offenders. The

first public playground in Chicago was the result
of a Hull-House experiment. Baths were provided and the great use made of them used as an
argument for municipal bathhouses. Co-opera-
tive enterprises ranged from coal purchasing to
an apartment house for working girls. The
Coffee House offered an alternative, if not a
substitute, for the saloon. Spurred on by experience with small children of working mothers,
Hull-House worked for Mother's pensions. Industrial medicine and the union label were born
there. Drama and music were used to integrate
immigrants into the community. Investigations
of all kinds—into housing, typhoid, tuberculosis,
drug addiction, prostitution, truancy—were in-
tiated. *Hull-House Maps and Papers* was an
early example of the use of social statistics and
now provides a unique source for the social and
economic historian of Chicago in the nineties.
The Rockford Summer School for Working
Girls provided a brief academic experience for
factory workers. Other settlements: the Chicago
Commons headed by Graham Taylor, the North-
western Settlement under Raymond Robbins and
Mary MacDowell's University of Chicago Settlement took inspiration from Hull-House.

Jane Addams was a strong believer in associated

effort, so Hull-House experimented with many clubs: boys, girls, Italian, German, Eight-Hour, Plato, Dante, Woman's Club, and—the one she liked best—the Working People's Social Science Club which gave a platform to any social or economic theory the members wanted to propound. She searched for educational experiments that might reach the mass of factory workers.

Money was scarce in the 1890's, but Jane Addams' own faith in her vision attracted support, and the House grew. The art gallery, the gymnasium, the coffee shop, the cooperative home for working girls, the Labor Museum were added.

The death rate in the nineteenth ward was much higher than the city average, and at least one obvious source of disease was the poor state of the garbage collection. In 1895 Jane Addams began to investigate the problem, with the result that she secured appointment as garbage inspector, and rose at six each morning to follow the collector upon his appointed rounds, much to the improvement of the ward and the fury of the collector.

Garbage collection was only one of the urgent problems. It was soon clear that philanthropy could not deal with unpaved streets, nonexistent school rooms, smallpox epidemics, four-year-old thread pullers and their sweated garment-worker parents. Only the state had the power and scope to be effective. It was natural that the residents of Hull-House should go into politics: ward politics, state politics, and eventually even national politics. Among them only Florence Kelley had ever been a doctrinaire socialist, but experience made the others increasingly radical. In 1904 Jane Addams wrote while on a trip to New York:

We see John Brown's farm and the flag flying over his grave. I have always had a secret sympathy with his impatience and his determination that something should . . . happen . . . I suppose the first martyrs of economic slavery will come from the city. If it depends on impatience I might be the one.[25]

This was a radicalism that began with experience, not with doctrine. What Hull-House residents saw around them made them early proponents of factory inspection and the regulation of wages, hours, and working conditions. They supported legislation to this end. Jane

[25] Jane Addams to Mary Rozet Smith, Aug. 1904, Swarthmore College Peace Collection.

INTRODUCTION

Addams became a crusader for the regulation of
child labor—both state and federal—and made
hundreds of speeches on the subject, enlisting
support wherever she could find it. Hull-House
became a haven for trade unionists and union
organizers.[26]

The residents were not long in finding themselves in conflict with the political boss of the
nineteenth ward, Alderman John Powers, who
stood next to "Hinky-Dink" McKenna and
"Bathhouse John" Coughlan in the hierarchy of
Chicago political corruption. In 1896 a member
of the Hull-House Men's Club was persuaded to
run for the ward's second seat on the Common
Council, but shortly after his election he was
bought out by Powers. In 1898 the residents
launched an all-out campaign to defeat Powers
himself. They succeeded in scaring him into
unaccustomed efforts in his own behalf, and the
nineteenth ward was soon sharing Chicago head-
lines with the sinking of the *Maine* in Havana
harbor. Powers won but by a reduced margin.
Jane Addams seems to have accepted the general
view that her own ward was one of the few in

[26] See Mary Anderson, *Woman at Work* (Madison, 1952), *passim*
and Agnes Nestor, *Woman's Labor Leader* (Rockford, 1954).

INTRODUCTION

which reform was impossible, and thereafter
transferred her political efforts to the city school
board and state and national reform.

Hull-House became, as Alice Hamilton would
say sixty years later, the most exciting place
in the world to live. It had a magnetic attraction
for foreign visitors, and even Beatrice Webb,
who found American society so depressing, noted
in her diary in 1898 that Hull-House was
"one continuous intellectual and emotional fer-
ment." [27]

In a very short time Jane Addams became a
subject of immense interest in Chicago, and
quickly thereafter in the country at large and in
other parts of the world. As early as 1893 on a
trip east, she was writing to her sister, "I find I am
considered quite the grandmother of American
settlements." [28] By the time she went to England in 1896 she was well known to all the leading reformers. After a small dinner at which
the Webbs had been the only other guests she
noted "there was a little reception afterward of
about twenty people, apparently all distinguished

[27] *Beatrice Webb's American Diary,* David Shannon, editor (Madison, 1963), p. 108.
[28] Jane Addams to Alice Haldeman, Feb. 23, 1893, Swarthmore
College Peace Collection.

for something." [29] In Paris in 1900 she ruefully
reported being treated as a "veteran" in social
reform.

A vignette of Jane Addams in 1899 has been
preserved in a letter from one of the residents to
Mary Smith who was abroad:

She is very tired . . . of course she did not let [that]
deter her from tearing about. She preached for the
Methodists last Sunday, entertained the Colored Women
of the National Council (Mrs. Booker Washington et
al) yesterday & later went to Winnetka . . . she runs
over to Mrs. Jones—around to Mrs. Fiellras . . up to
Mrs. Kenyon—off with Mrs. Haldemane, down to
inquiring strangers & in and out & around about to
Italian Fiestas, forced marriages, rows between scabs
& unions etc etc etc until my head spins & I sink exhausted while she poses to Mr. Linden [portrait painter]
& discusses the questions of the day with freshness &
calmness that put the finishing touches on my amaze-
ment. . . . Yesterday a committee from the Building
Trades Council waited upon her very courteously to
tell her that the mosaic workers now at last engaged on
the floor were "each & all" scabs & that the Union
plasterers (also working) would have to be called off
unless the others were. So I left the Lady starting for

[29] Jane Addams to Mary Rozet Smith, June 27, 1896, Swarthmore
College Peace Collection.

Mr. Pond's office while Mr. Linden folded up his tools in despair.[30]

ii

Both to raise money for Hull-House and to promote thinking on the subjects of her concern, Jane Addams lectured frequently in the nineties to all kinds of audiences. Once these lectures had been tried out a few times, she turned them into articles. In 1902 seven articles, which had appeared in periodicals ranging from *The Atlantic Monthly* to *The American Journal of Sociology* were gathered into her first book. *Democracy and Social Ethics* is a milestone in her intellectual biography; it lays down the general lines of thought which she would continue to develop for another forty years.

These articles reflect in various ways upon the subject which most fascinated Jane Addams, the effort to socialize democracy. Rejecting what she called the inadequate formulation of the eighteenth century which saw democracy largely in terms of the franchise, she thought the spiritual malaise of her own time called for a broader definition. Her own search had led to a few

---

[30] Gertrude Barnum to Mary Rozet Smith, Aug. 16, 1899, Swarthmore College Peace Collection.

simple ideas. One was a basic belief in the interdependence of all human beings. Another was confidence in the essential worth of *each* of them. But the individual could only be fully developed and make his full contribution in the framework of a society which recognized interdependence and techniques of associated action. Using her own version of the doctrine of evolution she reasoned that in an earlier step up from savagery man had evolved an ethic of individual goodness which, at the time, represented progress. Now the social organism had out-distanced ethical development and a new evolutionary step was demanded. Committed though she was to the idea of evolution she rejected entirely the Spencerian notion that evolution was automatic or that good automatically came from it. Like Lester Ward she injected mind and will into the process, and occasionally seemed to suggest that there was no particular virtue in being ethical when it was easy.

The demand for a sense of social responsibility was common in her time. Jane Addams' particular concern was the question of how a social ethic could evolve. With Tolstoy she felt that those who were trying to develop it needed to involve themselves in the social process. Other moralists might sit in their studies and meditate. Jane Addams would go to the corner of Polk and Halstead Streets and "drink at the great wells of human experience." By observing and grappling with the hardest practical problems of the confusing new urban society, she believed, one could begin to sense what evolution had in store.

It is legitimate to ask an ethical philosopher "How do we know what is good (or true)?" Jane Addams' response was: from experience. "We have come to have an enormous interest in human life as such accompanied by confidence in its essential soundness," she wrote. "We do not believe that genuine experience can lead us astray any more than scientific data can."

She thought her philosophy came from experience and that her basic drive had always been "the desire to live in a really living world and refusing to be content with a shadowy intellectual and aesthetic reflection of it."

There are several key elements in Jane Addams' thought: Darwinism, "experience," pragmatism, and personal value. Like most Darwinians she did not hesitate to impute her own values to the evolutionary process. The concept of "experience" played a central role in her thinking. It was the medium through which evolution was made clear. From it she was able to perceive certain patterns emerging, replacing others which she designated as "primitive," remnants of an earlier age. It was the idea of "experience" which allowed her to bridge the gap between fact and value, a use to which Dewey put the same concept. No more than other social Darwinists did she recognize the impossibility of deriving value from fact.

She examined the world about her in the light of a deeply held set of personal values and when she found it wanting, worked to change it. For example, the facts of urban life made the increasing interdependence of human beings visible. They did not prove that each member of society was of equal value or had an equal contribution to make to the common life. The first was observable fact, the second Jane Addams' value-laden interpretation. In the same way, when she found associative experiments arising among the immigrants or workingmen she did not hesitate to impute to these people inherently superior wisdom and goodness.

The Darwinian outlook served another and

more useful function in Jane Addams' thought. It engendered in her the valuable habit of being alert to the process of social change. When she referred to "experience" in this sense it was, as in the pragmatism of James and Dewey, a corrective to doctrine. With them she believed that ideas should not be judged true or false in themselves, but only on the basis of whether they worked in practice. There was no such thing as a "good" idea that worked badly. And an idea which might have been good in one set of circumstances might be bad in a new and different set. In this framework she looked at a number of social problems with which she was intimately familiar, and in each case saw the older individual ethical standards at war with a newer, emerging, social standard visible among the poorer people. The recipients of charity rather than the dispensers had developed, she argued, a genuine feeling for their interdependence; the trade unionists were developing techniques of associated action which modern industry so badly needed; hard-pressed factory women were finding ways to do without outmoded domestic service; the political boss rather than the patrician reformer represented the wave of the future in politics. It followed that if the poor were in the forefront of ethical development, social equality was essential to progress. Although in practice she and her associates recognized the need for leadership and that it might come from the upper as well as the working class, there is almost no mention of this in her theoretical analysis.

Through the whole of her early writing the glorification of the working class with its echoes of Comte (who had once written "The working class, then, is better qualified than any other for understanding and still more for sympathizing with the highest truths of morality") [31] existed side by side with keen observations and devastating realism which saw the failings of her immigrant neighbors as clearly as their virtues. Mysticism and realism combined with a fine sense of style account for some of her fascination.

The key to the chapter called "The Charitable Effort" may lie in a paragraph which appeared in the earlier version published in the *Atlantic Monthly* but was deleted in the book:

For most of the years during a decade of residence in a settlement, my mind was sore and depressed over the

---

[31] Auguste Comte, *A General View of the Positive Philosophy* (Paris, 1848), p. 151.

difficulties of the charitable relationship. The incessant clashing of ethical standards which had been honestly gained from varying industrial experience,—the misunderstandings inevitable between people whose conventions and mode of life had been so totally unlike,—made it seem reasonable to say that nothing could be done until industrial conditions were made absolutely democratic.

She then went on to say that after much reflection she had concluded that such direct experience with poverty was in any case the necessary forerunner if "individual sympathy and intelligence are [to be] caught into the forward intuitive movement of the mass . . . The social reformers who avoid the charitable relationship with any of their fellow men take a certain outside attitude to this movement. They may analyze and formulate it, but they are not essentially within it." [32]

In a complex industrial society, where many people were at the mercy of forces over which they had no control, charity in the traditional sense was really obsolete. Society as it was organized was creating needs greater than individual charity could handle. The crying need was for a new organization of society which would assure

[32] Jane Addams, "The Subtle Problems of Charity," *Atlantic Monthly*, 83:163–178 (Feb. 1899).

every member of it a decent wage and a chance to work. Such a change she suggests here and later in the chapter on "Industrial Amelioration" was likely to be brought about only by the victims of industrialization with the help of people like herself who were willing to immerse themselves in the problems of the masses. This opportunity to learn about the life of the masses was the function which the charitable relationship was still capable of serving.

In this chapter as in all the succeeding ones, the body of theory was brought to life with material drawn from experience and observation, presented with Jane Addams' considerable talent for identifying herself with any kind of person she was describing.

The essay "Filial Relations" was again presented in the pattern of conflict between an accepted and a newly emerging ethical standard, in this case the one lying at the heart of the woman movement. In the centuries before the industrial revolution the mere maintenance of family life required a woman's best energies. If she had skill at healing, her opportunities were great. Muscle and mind were required to provide food, clothing, shelter, and education for the young. In this social situation the belief that woman's place was in her home was sensible. But one by one meaningful responsibilities disappeared from the lives of well-to-do women. The public school, commercial farming, factory-made clothing, city life: each of these seemed good in itself, but for women the shell of homemaking remained while the substance, except for the care of small children, was removed. It was as if the upper-middle-class woman was herself drained of meaning and remained on the scene as a decorative doll. Thorstein Veblen had described the process from the outside in *The Theory of the Leisure Class*. Jane Addams looked at it from the inside. From her own experience and that of her closest friends she knew the inchoate sense of uselessness which afflicted young women of leisure; at the same time she saw around her endless work that women could and should do to meet pressing social needs. Could the world's expectation of women be modified to admit a new social ethic? She suggested that the needs of a growing community called for women to add to their traditional functions responsibility for social action. From her own experience she recognized that the assumption of community responsibility made emo-

tional as well as intellectual demands, and that a
woman who attempted to fill her traditional obligations as well as the newer ones might feel a
conflict.

To partly solve this problem she put forward
William James's notion that an emotion is weak-
ened by each successive failure to act upon it,
and argued that a girl who felt the impulse to
meet social needs but failed to act suffered a net
loss of energy. If this happened repeatedly health
might even give way.

The subject of this analysis was clearly the
well-educated single girl from a well-to-do family
upon whom there was no pressing demand to
earn a living and who, as a result of her education,
could no longer be content in the restricted traditional sphere of action. The descriptions here
were drawn from her own experience, and that
of Mary Rozet Smith, whose conflict concerning
her family tie and her desire to play an active
community role had been the subject of much
discussion between them.

The chapter called "Household Adjustment"
took up the role of women and the ethics of
family life versus those of society from another
angle. The servant problem was perennially dis-

cussed in America but Jane Addams took hold of it by a new handle. Pointing out that nearly all the industrial functions once carried on by the householder had been transferred to the factory or the skilled outside craftsman, she saw the live-in servant as an anachronism in the twentieth century. Most writers began from the point of how the function of the maid was to be filled in a relatively maidless society; Jane Addams began with the maid's own view of life and asked why she was so reluctant to enter domestic service. She identified herself so well with the servant girl that she often gave the impression that she had been a maid. In her analysis of the servant's discontent she anticipated conclusions reached in our day by researchers who have explained the lives of factory workers, that not the work itself or even its physical conditions determine satisfaction and output—but the sense of belonging and *esprit de corps.* The social ethic she called for would recognize the human needs of the servant as equal to those of the employer, and thus would dictate a determined effort to find new methods of household management which would emancipate the servant.

Early in her career Jane Addams had developed

a strong interest in the trade union movement. Union organizers were welcome at Hull-House, and though she occasionally became exasperated with particular ones, she steadfastly supported the principle of collective bargaining. In it she discerned one of the evolutionary currents she considered most vital, the development of new techniques of associated action.

Modern industry she thought to be on the wrong track because an inherently social effort was used for individual gain. It was not only that the profits of labor went largely to the capitalist, but even a well-meaning employer who attempted to give his workers certain benefits was going in the wrong direction. Doing things for people did not develop their capacities and contradicted the most basic meaning of social democracy. Experiments were needed to find ways for workers to help themselves. Industry needed to be reorganized so that decisions as well as profits could be shared. Only the unions, as far as she could see, were moving in the direction of a new type of industrial organization.

She did credit private initiative with useful experiments which might otherwise never be tried, but argued that once successful, such experiments must be transferred to an arena in which the workers could take part in the decision making if they were to have lasting value.

In the chapter on "Educational Methods" Jane Addams offered the extreme statement of her democratic faith when she asserted that not only was it the right of every man to have his full powers "freed" by education, but also that society was the loser when *any* citizen was not educated so that the moral power that was in him would be available. It was this moral power in all human beings which in this essay she identified as the engine of social change. Whether this was the Quaker "something of God in every man" or the Comtean insistence upon a mystic source of goodness in the working class, or simply Jane Addams' own faith in innate human goodness is of little moment. The point is that this was her ultimate faith, and the thing which kept her going at times when the concrete evidence might have led to the gravest doubts about human goodness.

It is not surprising, in the light of what has gone before, to find here also the idea that education should consciously train for social action. Educational patterns needed new structure to bring them into coherence with the kinds of lives people really lived. This discussion exposed Jane Addams' deep and often reiterated concern about the meaninglessness of industrial labor. Her observations of the effects of factory life and the division of labor on different personality types were acute. A great concern for production coupled with a lack of concern for the producer seemed to her immoral.

She wanted schools to do two things—first to relate what they taught to the life of the pupil, and second to help him see his place in the world in its relationship to the rest of society. A comparison with John Dewey's *School and Society*, published two years earlier, suggests the high degree of interaction in the thinking of these lifelong friends. Dewey had served on the Board of Hull-House and conducted some of his early experiments there. There are striking parallels between his book and this essay.

Jane Addams' theory of education is a natural corollary of her belief that social evolution would come from the working people. Therefore the educational system had to offer them full opportunity for personal development and a way of connecting themselves with the life of the community. She admitted that the settlement had not

yet found techniques of education which were
effective with the great mass of factory operatives.

The final chapter, "Political Reform," had first
appeared four years earlier, on the eve of the campaign to defeat Alderman Powers, under the im-
probable title "Some Ethical Survivals in Municipal Corruption." Anticipating Lincoln Steffens,
who began his research for *The Shame of the
Cities* just about the time *Democracy and Social
Ethics* was published, Jane Addams explained the
structure of the "boss's" power in an immigrant
community, and the emotional and practical basis
for it. She demonstrated in detail the ways in
which the boss made himself part of the "real
life of the community," while the reformer so
frequently concerned himself merely with ad-
ministrative purification. Politics, she said, was
not in an airtight compartment, unrelated to the
community. It was rather one of the modes
of expression of the basic moral habits of a
group of people. She pointed out that the corporate executive who found it cheaper to bribe the
alderman than to pay higher taxes was on the same
moral plane as the alderman who used his money
in turn to buy the support of his constituents. She
asserted flatly that in a democracy "all move for-

ward or retrograde together," and that therefore no single group could be pointed to as the source of community corruption. No one would have been more surprised than Alderman Powers to find Jane Addams saying:

> Would it be dangerous to conclude that the corrupt politician himself, because he is democratic in method, is on a more ethical line of social development than the reformer, who believes that people must be made over by "good citizens" and governed by "experts"? The former at least are engaged in that great moral effort of getting the mass to express itself, and of adding this mass energy and wisdom to the community as a whole.

The essay concluded with an emotional tribute to democracy which suggested that she had come to identify it with Christian fellowship.

Taken together these essays illuminate the underlying assumptions upon which Jane Addams' life as a social reformer, as well as her social theory, were grounded. They show how she combined observation and intuition in a framework of almost religious intensity and moral idealism. They also provide a commentary upon some of the problems of central concern to American progressives and English reformers and offer some illuminating social history.

INTRODUCTION

Though she never felt at home with any single-minded doctrine, Jane Addams was not afraid to be radical. Clearly a child of her times, of Darwin, James, and Dewey as well as of Ruskin, Comte, Toynbee, Frederick Maurice, and Charles Kingsley, she was also original and had a strong tendency to go to the heart of any problem, by intuition if not by reason. The validity of the questions she asked is suggested by their appropriateness after sixty years in the context of a struggle to move from an individual to a social ethic in race relations.

When the manuscript of *Democracy and Social Ethics* was in the hands of the publisher Jane Addams wrote to Mary Smith that she was in terrible throes about the "dreadful book" and wishing that she could do it over again. Once out, it received a chorus of praise, some perceptive, some not. Edward T. Devine, writing in *Charities*, took her charity visitor too literally, and accused her of setting up a straw man and then "demolishing an enemy that had already been routed." Charles R. Henderson in the *Journal of Sociology* came closer to the mark, and perhaps also answered Mr. Devine, when he wrote "The careless reader is likely to miss the point of view in this delicate and indirect treatment of our egoism."

Letters to her were enthusiastic. E. A. R. Seligman said that it was long since he had read "so sane and inspiring a book." Stanley McCormick wrote that he was planning an experiment in profit sharing. Fellow social workers thought she had said what they all knew but had not formulated, and Canon Barnett thought she helped "us see how if we boldly face what seems evil we see good . . ." [33] The reaction of the general public may be gauged by the fact that 1676 copies were sold in the first month and at the end of six weeks a second printing was necessary. The publishers were sufficiently pleased to urge her to write another book as soon as possible.

iii

When *Democracy and Social Ethics* appeared in 1902 Jane Addams was already working in most of the areas which it discussed. In the next dozen years she broadened her activity in many directions. She undertook a larger responsibility for the national woman suffrage campaign, served

[33] All these reviews and letters are in the Jane Addams Papers, Swarthmore College Peace Collection, letters dated May and June 1902.

on the Chicago School Board which was the center of far-reaching political and educational battles, took a hand in the national as well as the state campaign to outlaw child labor, served as mediator in labor disputes, helped to forge the historic agreement between Hart, Schaffner, and Marx and the Amalgamated Clothing Workers, was the first woman president of the National Conference of Charities and Corrections, helped to found the National Association for the Advancement of Colored People, helped edit the magazine *Charities* and its successor *The Survey*, and took a hand in the organization of the Progressive party. Even this list is not inclusive.

There was a constant interaction between her life and thought, and a stream of lectures and articles ultimately became books. In 1906 she published *Newer Ideals of Peace* building upon William James's idea of a moral substitute for war. Her approach to peace was indirect; she extended further the idea of a social ethic. She developed again her theory of the nascent social morality to be found in the crowded immigrant quarters, and argued that when this development was encouraged and directed, made really operative in society, the need for war would gradually disappear. It is something of a surprise, in view of the title, to turn to the book and find chapter headings such as "Immigrants in City Government," "Industrial Legislation," and "Group Morality." It is in fact an extension and expansion of *Democracy and Social Ethics,* with the difference that it projects the ideal of social morality upon the world scene.

Her next book, *The Spirit of Youth and the City Streets* (1909) was a major contribution to urban sociology (which, as a distinct field, did not appear for another sixteen years). It inspired William James to write that certain pages of it "seem to me quite immortal statements" and to add that

the wholeness of Miss Addams' embrace of life is her own secret.

She simply *inhabits reality* and everything she says necessarily expresses its nature. She can't help writing the truth.[34]

Hard upon the heels of *The Spirit of Youth* came the autobiographical *Twenty Years at Hull-House* (1910), one of the most widely read of all her books. The impulse to write it, she said, came partly because settlements had multiplied so easily in the United States that she hoped "a simple

[34] *The American Journal of Sociology,* 15:558.

statement of an earlier effort, including the stress and storm, might be of value in their interpretation and clear them of a certain charge of superficiality." Partly, also, she wanted to forestall two biographies of her which were in progress and which made life in the settlement "all too smooth and charming."

Warning that she was too close to the people and the causes she loved to treat them critically, she nevertheless managed to give a picture of the experiences of her first fifty years which constitutes social and intellectual history of a high order. Her earlier books, she said, constituted an effort to set forth a thesis, while this volume "endeavors to trace the experiences through which various conclusions were forced upon me." [35]

Two years later she published another important piece of urban analysis, *A New Conscience and an Ancient Evil*, a study of the economic origins of prostitution with, again, special reference to the youth of the cities. Published first serially in *McClure's,* it brought a flood of mail.

Until 1914 the development of Jane Addams' life and thought followed a logical pattern. This

[35] *Twenty Years at Hull-House*, viii, ix.

was still true, but less visibly so, after the outbreak of war. Like many other American liberals she had been horrified to see Europe move toward exactly the catastrophe which was no longer supposed to happen. She had been active in peace movements and her international ties through the settlement movement were strong. With the outbreak of hostilities she turned all her energy to efforts to bring the war to a speedy end. With Carrie Chapman Catt she issued a "call" for a convention in Washington in January 1915 which led to the formation of the Woman's Peace Party, an organization dedicated to finding a way to end the war and bring about an international organization to keep peace. In the spring of 1915 she journeyed to The Hague to preside over an International Congress of Women, made up of delegates from both the warring and neutral nations. This group later organized The Women's International League for Peace and Freedom, of which Jane Addams would be president until her death.

During the next two years she labored unceasingly to bring about a Conference of Neutrals to work out peace terms acceptable to all sides. She traveled with Alice Hamilton and Dr. Aletta Jacobs of Holland, to visit foreign ministers and leaders in many countries. She tried to persuade Woodrow Wilson, whose program seemed to parallel that of the Women's International League in many particulars, to seize the initiative in calling for an end to the war. Partly to this end she lent the weight of her name to the Democratic party in 1916.

Jane Addams' concept of pacifism was not a negative one. She was convinced that the horror of the war offered the strategic moment for a new breakthrough, that the time was ripe for an international government which could apply human intelligence to the solution of problems which, unsolved, led inexorably to war. Much of what she was proposing in 1916 and 1917 foreshadowed the economic and social work undertaken by the United Nations since 1945.

To her sorrow and dismay, after Wilson's re-election he seemed less and less inclined to follow the course she thought to be the only one which would help. After the Congress declared war in April 1917 she found herself increasingly unpopular. "Pacifist," which in 1914 had been a term of distinction, was now equated with German sympathizer or traitor. It was difficult for one whose convictions had not been changed as war fever swept the country to find a place to be useful. One by one fellow crusaders for peace decided that while war in general was bad, this war was necessary. Audiences which had cheered her now sat in stony silence. Old friends and colleagues took pains to dissociate themselves from her view.

Years later Ellen Starr paid tribute to the fact that when every hand seemed against her, and without even the comfort of self-righteousness, Jane Addams had continued to stand for peace in time of war. "All, even the great," Miss Starr wrote, "naturally enjoy the sunshine of approbation and work more easily in its congenial warmth. Jane Addams knew it well, and parted with it under no misconceptions; and what is more remarkable, no bitterness. She could not foresee that it would return." [36]

From two of her books, *Women at the Hague* (1915) and *Peace and Bread in Time of War* (1922), the high tragedy of these years emerges. Her own intelligence told her that human beings who were capable of effecting an international banking structure or the intricate web of international trade were not incapable of developing

[36] Ellen Gates Starr, Tribute prepared for Memorial Service organized by the National Federation of Settlements, June 1935, Sophia Smith Collection.

an international political system—if only they wanted to. Her extreme sensitivity to the value of human life made every death in the brutal and senseless battles a personal agony. Having tried with all her power, and with the support of thousands of women from many countries, to make governments see what she saw, and having failed, she was driven back into a kind of mysticism. The slogans about a war to end wars, to make the world safe for democracy, seemed to her wickedly wrong. How could anyone believe that good could come of such evil? Her old principle that the way in which a reform is brought about is as important as the reform itself was unshaken. It was impossible therefore for her to find the outlet available to most other Americans of throwing herself wholeheartedly into the war effort.

She could be wholehearted about the effort to feed the millions of people to whom war had brought hunger, and it was here that she tried to find some hope for the future. The traditional role of women, she said, had been to provide food for their children. Perhaps in the effort to feed other women's children in the warring countries American women might forge bonds of sympathy and faith which would transcend the enmity of governments and give hope for a new world in which nations would merge into an interconnected world state. It was a slender thread, but it gave her hope and thereby the energy to work unceasingly with Herbert Hoover's food program. Hoover, himself, was among those who stood by her during these trying years.[37]

To outsiders it probably seemed that Jane Addams' unpopularity dissipated when the war ended, and that in the twenties she was restored to the position of respect and in some cases almost veneration, which she had enjoyed before. From her own point of view the postwar years still held a good many trying experiences and *The Second Twenty Years at Hull-House* (1930) sounded a note of disillusionment which is different from anything in *Democracy and Social Ethics* or the original *Twenty Years*. To be accused of not being a loyal American because of her interest in developing a wider loyalty to an interdependent society seems occasionally to have caused her to despair of the wisdom of ordinary people in which she had so long put her faith. Few documents give so vivid a picture of the intol-

[37] Jane Addams, *Peace and Bread in Time of War* (New York, 1945), ch. iv.

erance which followed upon the excitement of the World War and the Palmer Red scare than her second autobiographical volume.

If she was less optimistic than in the days before 1914 she was not any less willing to engage in thought and action. The chapters in *The Second Twenty Years* range from the woman movement, prohibition, and immigrants to an analysis of the efforts to humanize justice and her old interest in the play instinct. A final chapter is a new formulation of her earlier idea of the propaganda of the deed: she calls it now "Education by the Current Event." Through it all there is no evidence of any diminution of intellectual energy. Nor is there any such evidence in her last volume, published posthumously, *My Friend Julia Lathrop* (1935), which tells a great deal about Jane Addams as well.

She continued to the end of her life a deep concern with international affairs and the effort to build the Women's International League for Peace and Freedom into an effective instrument for peace. In 1931 she shared the Nobel Peace Prize with Nicholas Murray Butler.

The depression brought new problems to her

door. Edmund Wilson went to Chicago in 1932 and wrote of Hull-House:

> Inside there is a peace and a sort of sanctity. Jane Addams at seventy-two still dominates her big house among the little ones . . . with her singular combination of the authority of a great lady and the humility of a saint . . . Through her vitality Hull-House still lives—the expression of both pride and humility: the pride of a moral vision which cannot accept as habitat any one of the little worlds of social and intellectual groupings; the humility of a spirit which, seeing so far, sees beyond itself, too, and feels itself lost amid the same uncertainties, thwarted by the same cross-purposes, as all of those struggling others.[38]

In 1935 to a large gathering held in her honor in Washington, describing the contemporary crisis she used a phrase very reminiscent of *Democracy and Social Ethics:* "The source of our difficulties lies in a lack of moral enterprise.[39] A few days later she died, and was honored in death as few private citizens have been.

Jane Addams' seventy-four years, stretching from 1860 to 1934, encompassed the most rapid and acute changes American history had then

[38] Edmund Wilson, *The American Earthquake* (New York, 1958), p. 454.
[39] Jane Addams, *A Centennial Reader* (New York, 1960), p. 325.

witnessed. Born a pioneer's child in a simple rural home, she died first citizen of Chicago, which had become a great city in the course of her lifetime.

There are no calipers exact enough to measure a life. Jane Addams was so many-sided that even the close student is apt to feel that he has missed something. But the major lines are reasonably clear. A talented youngster, she early developed a sense of destiny but was not sure what that destiny was. At Rockford, she showed signs of unusual personal magnetism. A missionary's life was urged upon her, but while she was deeply concerned with religion she could not accept orthodoxy. She began the long process of working out her own religion which, once accomplished, would provide the framework for her career. The death of a beloved father caused a spiritual crisis, followed by eight years of agonizing indecision. A mystical experience banished the indecision, and afterwards she was concentrated and effective, rapidly becoming a leader, a teacher and a charismatic figure. The missionary career she had rejected was transmuted into a new form, and she became in the broad sense a religious leader and a saint.

In practice and in thought she boldly confronted the nineteenth century's most burdensome legacies to the twentieth: can human beings live in a rapidly changing industrial society and remain human? Can nations learn to live together in peace? Until she was fifty-four her attention was primarily on the first; for the remaining years on the second.

Herself a thoroughgoing evolutionist, from Hull-House she boldly attacked the dragon of Spencerian Darwinism. To rigid dogma she replied with a call for experience; to fatalism about the condition of the poor she opposed action; turning the social Darwinians' environmentalism back upon them she argued that the poor, far from being born "unfit," were a product of their environment. If it could be changed, so could they. The social Darwinists had no place for ethics; she called for a social morality, saying that an idea had to be judged by its consequences and that there was no such thing as a good idea that brought bad results. And she added for good measure that it was quite as necessary to have good means as good ends. Perhaps more important than anything else she was not content to preach: with her, indeed, preaching followed practice and therefore she could point to concrete accomplishment as proof, by her own pragmatic standard, of the worth of her ideas.

People loved her and she attracted many disciples. Partly this may have been because saintly figures are always rare, and in them we sense the dimly seen possibilities of the human condition. Partly it may have been her gift for communication and capacity to identify with almost any other person. She dealt effectively with practical questions and things unseen. She managed to encompass qualities which are often separated: she was saintly and an administrator; she was a thinker who was also a doer; a skilled critic who was also capable of constructive thought. She was at home discussing the largest questions of social policy, or dealing with the poorest inhabitant of the nineteenth ward, a seeker after truth who did not find the details of garbage collection beneath her.

The pacifism which became the primary theme of her last quarter-century was an outgrowth of her main concerns in the first fifty years. Having worked to help the hungry earn their bread, to save the children from physical and emotional deprivation, she could not quietly watch them sent off to be killed. She saw war as a historical anachronism, a measure of the human failure to develop a full understanding of the social nature of goodness, a lack of moral enterprise. Her rejection of war was basic and not unlike that of the other figures with whom she may justly be compared: St. Francis, Gandhi, and Tolstoy. Tolstoy found the key to life in the single sentence, "Resist not evil." Jane Addams understood this, and practiced it, but added to it "Love thy neighbor as thyself."

As much as any member of her generation she contributed to that evolution of social conscience which she so longed to see take place, as the necessary precondition to social change. This may be her most enduring legacy, though her socialization of women's role and her practical social inventions to meet the problems of the urban world reach deep into contemporary life and have in turn created new questions which this generation must answer.

Her own words written about William Penn form a fitting summary:

Such right thinking and courageous action in the life of one man has an enormous liberating power and taps new sources of human energy. It is doubtless what we need at this moment more than anything else, a generous and fearless desire to see life as it is, irrespective of the limitations and traditions which so needlessly divide us.[40]

[40] Jane Addams, "The Social Deterrent of Our National Self-Consciousness," *Survey Graphic*, 22:98–101 (Feb. 1933).

A NOTE ON THE TEXT

Democracy and Social Ethics remained in print under the publication of The Macmillan Company of New York from 1902 until 1926, precisely in its original form. The present edition is a photographic reproduction of a 1907 copy in superior condition. Under the copyright notice the 1907 copy carries this bibliographic note: "Set up and electrotyped March, 1902. Reprinted June, September, 1902; August, 1905; November, 1907." The publisher has no record of the number of subsequent printings of the book.

Quotations in the Editor's Introduction from the correspondence of Ellen Gates Starr with Jane Addams and others, from the Sophia Smith Collection, are available through the courtesy of the Smith College Library. Other manuscript quotations, from the Jane Addams Papers, are available through the courtesy of the curator of the Swarthmore College Peace Collection.

DEMOCRACY AND SOCIAL ETHICS

BY

JANE ADDAMS

HULL-HOUSE, CHICAGO

New York
THE MACMILLAN COMPANY
LONDON: MACMILLAN & CO., Ltd.

1907

To M. R. S.

PREFATORY NOTE

THE following pages present the substance of a course of twelve lectures on "Democracy and Social Ethics" which have been delivered at various colleges and university extension centres.

In putting them into the form of a book, no attempt has been made to change the somewhat informal style used in speaking. The "we" and "us" which originally referred to the speaker and her audience are merely extended to possible readers.

Acknowledgment for permission to reprint is extended to *The Atlantic Monthly*, *The International Journal of Ethics*, *The American Journal of Sociology*, and to *The Commons*.

DEMOCRACY AND SOCIAL ETHICS

CHAPTER I

INTRODUCTION

IT is well to remind ourselves, from time to time, that " Ethics " is but another word for "righteousness," that for which many men and women of every generation have hungered and thirsted, and without which life becomes meaningless.

Certain forms of personal righteousness have become to a majority of the community almost automatic. It is as easy for most of us to keep from stealing our dinners as it is to digest them, and there is quite as much voluntary morality involved in one process as in the other. To steal would be for us to fall sadly below the standard of habit and expectation which makes virtue easy. In the same way we have been carefully reared to a sense

of family obligation, to be kindly and consid-
erate to the members of our own households,
and to feel responsible for their well-being.
As the rules of conduct have become established in regard to our self-development and
our families, so they have been in regard to
limited circles of friends. If the fulfilment
of these claims were all that a righteous life
required, the hunger and thirst would be
stilled for many good men and women, and
the clew of right living would lie easily in
their hands.

But we all know that each generation has
its own test, the contemporaneous and current standard by which alone it can adequately judge of its own moral achievements,
and that it may not legitimately use a previous and less vigorous test. The advanced
test must indeed include that which has
already been attained; but if it includes no
more, we shall fail to go forward, thinking
complacently that we have "arrived" when
in reality we have not yet started.

To attain individual morality in an age

demanding social morality, to pride one's self on the results of personal effort when the time demands social adjustment, is utterly to fail to apprehend the situation.

It is perhaps significant that a German critic has of late reminded us that the one test which the most authoritative and dramatic portrayal of the Day of Judgment offers, is the social test. The stern questions are not in regard to personal and family relations, but did ye visit the poor, the criminal, the sick, and did ye feed the hungry?

All about us are men and women who have become unhappy in regard to their attitude toward the social order itself; toward the dreary round of uninteresting work, the pleasures narrowed down to those of appetite, the declining consciousness of brain power, and the lack of mental food which characterizes the lot of the large proportion of their fellow-citizens. These men and women have caught a moral challenge raised by the exigencies of contemporaneous life; some are bewildered, others who are denied

3

the relief which sturdy action brings are even seeking an escape, but all are increasingly anxious concerning their actual relations to the basic organization of society.

The test which they would apply to their conduct is a social test. They fail to be content with the fulfilment of their family and personal obligations, and find themselves striving to respond to a new demand involving a social obligation; they have become conscious of another requirement, and the contribution they would make is toward a code of social ethics. The conception of life which they hold has not yet expressed itself in social changes or legal enactment, but rather in a mental attitude of maladjustment, and in a sense of divergence between their consciences and their conduct. They desire both a clearer definition of the code of morality adapted to present day demands and a part in its fulfilment, both a creed and a practice of social morality. In the perplexity of this intricate situation at least one thing is becoming clear: if the latter day moral ideal is in reality that of a social morality, it is inevitable that those who desire it must be brought in contact with the moral experiences of the many in order to procure an adequate social motive.

These men and women have realized this and have disclosed the fact in their eagerness for a wider acquaintance with and participation in the life about them. They believe that experience gives the easy and trustworthy impulse toward right action in the broad as well as in the narrow relations. We may indeed imagine many of them saying: " Cast our experiences in a larger mould if our lives are to be animated by the larger social aims. We have met the obligations of our family life, not because we had made resolutions to that end, but spontaneously, because of a common fund of memories and affections, from which the obligation naturally develops, and we see no other way in which to prepare ourselves for the larger social duties." Such a demand is reasonable, for by our daily experience we have discovered that we cannot mechanically hold up a moral standard, then jump at it in rare moments of exhilaration when we have the strength for it, but that even as the ideal itself must be a rational development of life, so the strength to attain it must be secured from interest in life itself. We slowly learn that life consists of processes as well as results, and that failure may come quite as easily from ignoring the adequacy of one's method as from selfish or ignoble aims. We are thus brought to a conception of Democracy not merely as a sentiment which desires the well-being of all men, nor yet as a creed which believes in the essential dignity and equality of all men, but as that which affords a rule of living as well as a test of faith.

We are learning that a standard of social ethics is not attained by travelling a sequestered byway, but by mixing on the thronged and common road where all must turn out for one another, and at least see the size of one another's burdens. To follow the path of social morality results perforce in the temper if not the practice of the democratic spirit, for it implies that diversified human experience and resultant sympathy which are the foundation and guarantee of Democracy.

There are many indications that this conception of Democracy is growing among us. We have come to have an enormous interest in human life as such, accompanied by confidence in its essential soundness. We do not believe that genuine experience can lead us astray any more than scientific data can.

We realize, too, that social perspective and sanity of judgment come only from contact with social experience; that such contact is the surest corrective of opinions concerning the social order, and concerning efforts, however humble, for its improvement. Indeed, it is a consciousness of the illuminating and dynamic value of this wider and more thorough human experience which explains in no small degree that new curiosity regarding human life which has more of a moral basis than an intellectual one.

The newspapers, in a frank reflection of popular demand, exhibit an omniverous curiosity equally insistent upon the trivial and the important. They are perhaps the most obvious manifestations of that desire to know, that "What is this?" and "Why do you do that?" of the child. The first dawn of the social consciousness takes this form, as the dawning intelligence of the child takes the form of constant question and insatiate curiosity.

Literature, too, portrays an equally absorbing though better adjusted desire to know all kinds of life. The popular books are the novels, dealing with life under all possible conditions, and they are widely read not only because they are entertaining, but also because they in a measure satisfy an unformulated belief that to see farther, to know all sorts of men, in an indefinite way, is a preparation for better social adjustment — for the remedying of social ills.

Doubtless one under the conviction of
sin in regard to social ills finds a vague
consolation in reading about the lives of
the poor, and derives a sense of complicity
in doing good. He likes to feel that he
knows about social wrongs even if he
does not remedy them, and in a very
genuine sense there is a foundation for
this belief.

Partly through this wide reading of
human life, we find in ourselves a new
affinity for all men, which probably never
existed in the world before. Evil itself does
not shock us as it once did, and we count
only that man merciful in whom we recognize an understanding of the criminal. We
have learned as common knowledge that
much of the insensibility and hardness of
the world is due to the lack of imagination
which prevents a realization of the experiences of other people. Already there is
a conviction that we are under a moral
obligation in choosing our experiences, since
the result of those experiences must ulti-

mately determine our understanding of life.
We know instinctively that if we grow con-
temptuous of our fellows, and consciously
limit our intercourse to certain kinds of
people whom we have previously decided
to respect, we not only tremendously cir-
cumscribe our range of life, but limit the
scope of our ethics.

We can recall among the selfish people
of our acquaintance at least one common
characteristic,—the conviction that they are
different from other men and women, that
they need peculiar consideration because
they are more sensitive or more refined.
Such people "refuse to be bound by any
relation save the personally luxurious ones
of love and admiration, or the identity of
political opinion, or religious creed." We
have learned to recognize them as selfish,
although we blame them not for the will
which chooses to be selfish, but for a narrowness of interest which deliberately selects
its experience within a limited sphere, and
we say that they illustrate the danger of

concentrating the mind on narrow and unprogressive issues.

We know, at last, that we can only discover truth by a rational and democratic
interest in life, and to give truth complete
social expression is the endeavor upon which
we are entering. Thus the identification
with the common lot which is the essential
idea of Democracy becomes the source and
expression of social ethics. It is as though
we thirsted to drink at the great wells of
human experience, because we knew that a
daintier or less potent draught would not
carry us to the end of the journey, going
forward as we must in the heat and jostle
of the crowd.

The six following chapters are studies of
various types and groups who are being
impelled by the newer conception of Democracy to an acceptance of social obligations
involving in each instance a new line of
conduct. No attempt is made to reach a
conclusion, nor to offer advice beyond the
assumption that the cure for the ills of

Democracy is more Democracy, but the quite unlooked-for result of the studies would seem to indicate that while the strain and perplexity of the situation is felt most keenly by the educated and self-conscious members of the community, the tentative and actual attempts at adjustment are largely coming through those who are simpler and less analytical.

CHAPTER II

CHARITABLE EFFORT

ALL those hints and glimpses of a larger and more satisfying democracy, which literature and our own hopes supply, have a tendency to slip away from us and to leave us sadly unguided and perplexed when we attempt to act upon them.

Our conceptions of morality, as all our other ideas, pass through a course of development; the difficulty comes in adjusting our conduct, which has become hardened into customs and habits, to these changing moral conceptions. When this adjustment is not made, we suffer from the strain and indecision of believing one hypothesis and acting upon another.

Probably there is no relation in life which our democracy is changing more rapidly than the charitable relation — that relation which obtains between benefactor and beneficiary; at the same time there is no point of contact in our modern experience which reveals so clearly the lack of that equality which democracy implies. We have reached the moment when democracy has made such inroads upon this relationship, that the complacency of the old-fashioned charitable man is gone forever; while, at the same time, the very need and existence of charity, denies us the consolation and freedom which democracy will at last give.

It is quite obvious that the ethics of none of us are clearly defined, and we are continually obliged to act in circles of habit, based upon convictions which we no longer hold. Thus our estimate of the effect of environment and social conditions has doubtless shifted faster than our methods of administrating charity have changed. Formerly when it was believed that poverty was synonymous with vice and laziness, and that

the prosperous man was the righteous man
charity was administered harshly with a
good conscience; for the charitable agent
really blamed the individual for his poverty, and the very fact of his own superior
prosperity gave him a certain consciousness
of superior morality. We have learned
since that time to measure by other standards, and have ceased to accord to the
money-earning capacity exclusive respect;
while it is still rewarded out of all proportion to any other, its possession is by no
means assumed to imply the possession of
the highest moral qualities. We have
learned to judge men by their social virtues
as well as by their business capacity, by
their devotion to intellectual and disinterested aims, and by their public spirit, and
we naturally resent being obliged to judge
poor people so solely upon the industrial
side. Our democratic instinct instantly
takes alarm. It is largely in this modern
tendency to judge all men by one democratic standard, while the old charitable

attitude commonly allowed the use of two standards, that much of the difficulty adheres. We know that unceasing bodily toil becomes wearing and brutalizing, and our position is totally untenable if we judge large numbers of our fellows solely upon their success in maintaining it.

The daintily clad charitable visitor who steps into the little house made untidy by the vigorous efforts of her hostess, the washerwoman, is no longer sure of her superiority to the latter; she recognizes that her hostess after all represents social value and industrial use, as over against her own parasitic cleanliness and a social standing attained only through status.

The only families who apply for aid to the charitable agencies are those who have come to grief on the industrial side; it may be through sickness, through loss of work, or for other guiltless and inevitable reasons; but the fact remains that they are industrially ailing, and must be bolstered and helped into industrial health. The charity visitor,

let us assume, is a young college woman,
well-bred and open-minded; when she visits
the family assigned to her, she is often em-
barrassed to find herself obliged to lay all
the stress of her teaching and advice upon
the industrial virtues, and to treat the members of the family almost exclusively as
factors in the industrial system. She insists that they must work and be self-
supporting, that the most dangerous of all
situations is idleness, that seeking one's
own pleasure, while ignoring claims and
responsibilities, is the most ignoble of
actions. The members of her assigned
family may have other charms and virtues
— they may possibly be kind and consider-
ate of each other, generous to their friends,
but it is her business to stick to the industrial side. As she daily holds up these
standards, it often occurs to the mind of
the sensitive visitor, whose conscience has
been made tender by much talk of brotherhood and equality, that she has no right
to say these things; that her untrained

hands are no more fitted to cope with actual conditions than those of her broken-down family.

The grandmother of the charity visitor could have done the industrial preaching very well, because she did have the industrial virtues and housewifely training. In a generation our experiences have changed, and our views with them; but we still keep on in the old methods, which could be applied when our consciences were in line with them, but which are daily becoming more difficult as we divide up into people who work with their hands and those who do not. The charity visitor belonging to the latter class is perplexed by recognitions and suggestions which the situation forces upon her. Our democracy has taught us to apply our moral teaching all around, and the moralist is rapidly becoming so sensitive that when his life does not exemplify his ethical convictions, he finds it difficult to preach.

Added to this is a consciousness, in the

mind of the visitor, of a genuine misunderstanding of her motives by the recipients of her charity, and by their neighbors. Let us take a neighborhood of poor people, and test their ethical standards by those of the charity visitor, who comes with the best desire in the world to help them out of their distress. A most striking incongruity, at once apparent, is the difference between the emotional kindness with which relief is given by one poor neighbor to another poor neighbor, and the guarded care with which relief is given by a charity visitor to a charity recipient. The neighborhood mind is at once confronted not only by the difference of method, but by an absolute clashing of two ethical standards.

A very little familiarity with the poor districts of any city is sufficient to show how primitive and genuine are the neighborly relations. There is the greatest willingness to lend or borrow anything, and all the residents of the given tenement know the most intimate family affairs of all the others.

The fact that the economic condition of all alike is on a most precarious level makes the ready outflow of sympathy and material assistance the most natural thing in the world. There are numberless instances of self-sacrifice quite unknown in the circles where greater economic advantages make that kind of intimate knowledge of one's neighbors impossible. An Irish family in which the man has lost his place, and the woman is struggling to eke out the scanty savings by day's work, will take in the widow and her five children who have been turned into the street, without a moment's reflection upon the physical discomforts involved. The most maligned landlady who lives in the house with her tenants is usually ready to lend a scuttle full of coal to one of them who may be out of work, or to share her supper. A woman for whom the writer had long tried in vain to find work failed to appear at the appointed time when employment was secured at last. Upon investigation it transpired that a neighbor further down the street was taken ill, that the children ran for the family friend, who went of course, saying simply when reasons for her non-appearance were demanded, " It broke me heart to leave the place, but what could I do?" A woman whose husband was sent up to the city prison for the maximum term, just three months, before the birth of her child found herself penniless at the end of that time, having gradually sold her supply of household furniture. She took refuge with a friend whom she supposed to be living in three rooms in another part of town. When she arrived, however, she discovered that her friend's husband had been out of work so long that they had been reduced to living in one room. The friend, however, took her in, and the friend's husband was obliged to sleep upon a bench in the park every night for a week, which he did uncomplainingly if not cheerfully. Fortunately it was summer, " and it only rained one night." The writer could not discover from the young mother that she had any special claim upon the "friend" beyond the fact that they had formerly worked together in the same factory. The husband she had never seen until the night of her arrival, when he at once went forth in search of a midwife who would consent to come upon his promise of future payment.

The evolutionists tell us that the instinct to pity, the impulse to aid his fellows, served man at a very early period, as a rude rule of right and wrong. There is no doubt that this rude rule still holds among many people with whom charitable agencies are brought into contact, and that their ideas of right and wrong are quite honestly outraged by the methods of these agencies. When they see the delay and caution with which relief is given, it does not appear to them a conscientious scruple, but as the cold and calculating action of a selfish man. It is not the aid that they are accustomed to receive from their neighbors, and they do not understand why the impulse which drives people to "be good to the poor" should be so severely supervised. They feel, remotely, that the charity visitor is moved by motives that are alien and unreal. They may be superior motives, but they are different, and they are "agin nature." They cannot comprehend why a person whose intellectual perceptions are stronger than his natural impulses, should go into charity work at all. The only man they are accustomed to see whose intellectual perceptions are stronger than his tenderness of heart, is the selfish and avaricious man who is frankly "on the make." If the charity visitor is such a person, why does she pretend to like the poor? Why does she not go into business at once?

We may say, of course, that it is a primitive view of life, which thus confuses intellectuality and business ability; but it is a view quite honestly held by many poor people who are obliged to receive charity from time to time. In moments of indignation the poor have been known to say: "What do you want, anyway? If you have nothing to give us, why not let us alone and stop your questionings and investigations?" "They investigated me for three weeks, and in the end gave me nothing but a black character," a little woman has been heard to assert. This indignation, which is for the most part taciturn, and a certain kindly contempt for her abilities, often puzzles the charity visitor. The latter may be explained by the standard of worldly success which the visited families hold. Success does not ordinarily go, in the minds of the poor, with charity and kind-heartedness, but rather with the opposite qualities. The rich landlord is he who collects with sternness, who accepts no excuse, and will have his own. There are moments of irritation and of real bitterness against him, but there is still admiration, because he is rich and successful. The good-natured landlord, he who pities and spares his poverty-pressed tenants, is seldom rich. He often lives in the back of his house, which he has owned for a long time, perhaps has inherited; but he has been able to accumulate little. He commands the genuine love and devotion of many a poor soul, but he is treated with a certain lack of respect. In one sense he is a failure. The charity visitor, just because she is a person who concerns herself with the poor, receives a certain amount of this good-natured and kindly contempt, sometimes real affection, but little genuine respect. The poor are accustomed to help each other and to respond according to their kindliness; but when it comes to worldly judgment, they use industrial success as the sole standard. In the case of the charity visitor who has neither natural kindness nor dazzling riches, they are deprived of both standards, and they find it of course utterly impossible to judge of the motive of organized charity.

Even those of us who feel most sorely the need of more order in altruistic effort and see the end to be desired, find something distasteful in the juxtaposition of the words "organized" and "charity." We say in defence that we are striving to turn this emotion into a motive, that pity is capricious, and not to be depended on; that we mean to give it the dignity of conscious duty. But at bottom we distrust a little a scheme which substitutes a theory of social conduct for the natural promptings of the heart, even although we appreciate the complexity of the situation. The poor man who has fallen into distress, when he first asks aid, instinctively expects tenderness, consideration, and forgiveness. If it is the first time, it has taken him long to make up his mind to take the step. He comes somewhat bruised and battered, and instead of being met with warmth of heart and sympathy, he is at once chilled by an investigation and an intimation that he ought to work. He does not recognize the disciplinary aspect of the situation.

The only really popular charity is that of the visiting nurses, who by virtue of their professional training render services which may easily be interpreted into sympathy and kindness, ministering as they do to obvious needs which do not require investigation.

The state of mind which an investigation arouses on both sides is most unfortunate; but the perplexity and clashing of different standards, with the consequent misunderstandings, are not so bad as the moral deterioration which is almost sure to follow.

When the agent or visitor appears among the poor, and they discover that under certain conditions food and rent and medical aid are dispensed from some unknown source, every man, woman, and child is quick to learn what the conditions may be, and to follow them. Though in their eyes a glass of beer is quite right and proper when taken as any self-respecting man should take it; though they know that cleanliness is an expensive virtue which can be required of few; though they realize that saving is well-nigh impossible when but a few cents can be laid by at a time; though their feeling for the church may be something quite elusive of definition and quite apart from daily living: to the visitor they gravely laud temperance and cleanliness and thrift

and religious observance. The deception
in the first instances arises from a wondering inability to understand the ethical ideals
which can require such impossible virtues,
and from an innocent desire to please. It
is easy to trace the development of the
mental suggestions thus received. When
A discovers that B, who is very little worse
off than he, receives good things from an
inexhaustible supply intended for the poor
at large, he feels that he too has a claim for
his share, and step by step there is developed
the competitive spirit which so horrifies
charity visitors when it shows itself in
a tendency to "work" the relief-giving
agencies.

The most serious effect upon the poor
comes when dependence upon the charitable society is substituted for the natural
outgoing of human love and sympathy,
which, happily, we all possess in some degree. The spontaneous impulse to sit up
all night with the neighbor's sick child is
turned into righteous indignation against

the district nurse, because she goes home at six o'clock, and doesn't do it herself. Or the kindness which would have prompted the quick purchase of much needed medicine is transformed into a voluble scoring of the dispensary, because it gives prescriptions and not drugs; and "who can get well on a piece of paper?"

If a poor woman knows that her neighbor next door has no shoes, she is quite willing to lend her own, that her neighbor may go decently to mass, or to work; for she knows the smallest item about the scanty wardrobe, and cheerfully helps out. When the charity visitor comes in, all the neighbors are baffled as to what her circumstances may be. They know she does not need a new pair of shoes, and rather suspect that she has a dozen pairs at home; which, indeed, she sometimes has. They imagine untold stores which they may call upon, and her most generous gift is considered niggardly, compared with what she might do. She ought to get new shoes for the family all round, "she sees well enough that they need them." It is no more than the neighbor herself would do, has practically done, when she lent her own shoes. The charity visitor has broken through the natural rule of giving, which, in a primitive society, is bounded only by the need of the recipient and the resources of the giver; and she gets herself into untold trouble when she is judged by the ethics of that primitive society.

The neighborhood understands the selfish rich people who stay in their own part of town, where all their associates have shoes and other things. Such people don't bother themselves about the poor; they are like the rich landlords of the neighborhood experience. But this lady visitor, who pretends to be good to the poor, and certainly does talk as though she were kind-hearted, what does she come for, if she does not intend to give them things which are so plainly needed?

The visitor says, sometimes, that in holding her poor family so hard to a standard of thrift she is really breaking down a rule of higher living which they formerly possessed; that saving, which seems quite commendable in a comfortable part of town, appears almost criminal in a poorer quarter where the next-door neighbor needs food, even if the children of the family do not.

She feels the sordidness of constantly being obliged to urge the industrial view of life. The benevolent individual of fifty years ago honestly believed that industry and self-denial in youth would result in comfortable possessions for old age. It was, indeed, the method he had practised in his own youth, and by which he had probably obtained whatever fortune he possessed. He therefore reproved the poor family for indulging their children, urged them to work long hours, and was utterly untouched by many scruples which afflict the contemporary charity visitor. She says sometimes, "Why must I talk always of getting work and saving money, the things

I know nothing about? If it were anything else I had to urge, I could do it; anything like Latin prose, which I had worried through myself, it would not be so hard." But she finds it difficult to connect the experiences of her youth with the experiences of the visited family.

Because of this diversity in experience, the visitor is continually surprised to find that the safest platitude may be challenged. She refers quite naturally to the "horrors of the saloon," and discovers that the head of her visited family does not connect them with "horrors" at all. He remembers all the kindnesses he has received there, the free lunch and treating which goes on, even when a man is out of work and not able to pay up; the loan of five dollars he got there when the charity visitor was miles away and he was threatened with eviction. He may listen politely to her reference to "horrors," but considers it only "temperance talk."

The charity visitor may blame the women

for lack of gentleness toward their children, for being hasty and rude to them, until she learns that the standard of breeding is not that of gentleness toward the children so much as the observance of certain conventions, such as the punctilious wearing of mourning garments after the death of a child. The standard of gentleness each mother has to work out largely by herself, assisted only by the occasional shame-faced remark of a neighbor, " That they do better when you are not too hard on them"; but the wearing of mourning garments is sustained by the definitely expressed sentiment of every woman in the street. The mother would have to bear social blame, a certain social ostracism, if she failed to comply with that requirement. It is not comfortable to outrage the conventions of those among whom we live, and, if our social life be a narrow one, it is still more difficult. The visitor may choke a little when she sees the lessened supply of food and the scanty clothing provided for the remaining children in order that one may be conventionally mourned, but she doesn't talk so strongly against it as she would have done during her first month of experience with the family since bereaved.

The subject of clothes indeed perplexes the visitor constantly, and the result of her reflections may be summed up somewhat in this wise: The girl who has a definite social standing, who has been to a fashionable school or to a college, whose family live in a house seen and known by all her friends and associates, may afford to be very simple, or even shabby as to her clothes, if she likes. But the working girl, whose family lives in a tenement, or moves from one small apartment to another, who has little social standing and has to make her own place, knows full well how much habit and style of dress has to do with her position. Her income goes into her clothing, out of all proportion to the amount which she spends upon other things. But, if social advancement is her aim, it is the most sensible thing she can do. She is judged largely by her clothes. Her house furnishing, with its pitiful little decorations, her scanty supply of books, are never seen by the people whose social opinions she most values. Her clothes are her background, and from them she is largely judged. It is due to this fact that girls' clubs succeed best in the business part of town, where "working girls" and "young ladies" meet upon an equal footing, and where the clothes superficially look very much alike. Bright and ambitious girls will come to these down-town clubs to eat lunch and rest at noon, to study all sorts of subjects and listen to lectures, when they might hesitate a long time before joining a club identified with their own neighborhood, where they would be judged not solely on their own merits and the unconscious social standing afforded by good clothes, but by other surroundings which are not nearly up to these. For the same reason, girls' clubs are infinitely more difficult to organize in little towns and villages, where every one knows every one else, just how the front parlor is furnished, and the amount of mortgage there is upon the house. These facts get in the way of a clear and unbiassed judgment; they impede the democratic relationship and add to the self-consciousness of all concerned. Every one who has had to do with down-town girls' clubs has had the experience of going into the home of some bright, well-dressed girl, to discover it uncomfortable and perhaps wretched, and to find the girl afterward carefully avoiding her, although the working girl may not have been at home when the call was made, and the visitor may have carried herself with the utmost courtesy throughout. In some very successful down-town clubs the home address is not given at all, and only the "business address" is required. Have we worked out our democracy further in regard to clothes than anything else?

The charity visitor has been rightly brought up to consider it vulgar to spend much money upon clothes, to care so much for "appearances." She realizes dimly that the care for personal decoration over that for one's home or habitat is in some way primitive and undeveloped; but she is silenced by its obvious need. She also catches a glimpse of the fact that the disproportionate expenditure of the poor in the matter of clothes is largely due to the exclusiveness of the rich who hide from them the interior of their houses, and their more subtle pleasures, while of necessity exhibiting their street clothes and their street manners. Every one who goes shopping at the same time may see the clothes of the richest women in town, but only those invited to her receptions see the Corot on her walls or the bindings in her library. The poor naturally try to bridge the difference by reproducing the street clothes which they have seen. They are striving to conform to a common standard which their democratic training presupposes belongs to all of us. The charity visitor may regret that the Italian peasant woman has laid aside her picturesque kerchief and substituted a cheap street hat. But it is easy to recognize the first attempt toward democratic expression.

The charity visitor finds herself still more perplexed when she comes to consider such problems as those of early marriage and child labor; for she cannot deal with them according to economic theories, or according to the conventions which have regulated her own life. She finds both of these fairly upset by her intimate knowledge of the situation, and her sympathy for those into whose lives she has gained a curious insight. She discovers how incorrigibly bourgeois her standards have been, and it takes but a little time to reach the conclusion that she cannot insist so strenuously upon the conventions of her own class, which fail to fit the bigger, more emotional, and freer lives of working people. The charity visitor holds well-grounded views upon the imprudence of early marriages, quite naturally because she comes from a family and circle of professional and business people. A professional man is scarcely equipped and started in his profession before he is thirty. A business man, if he is on the road to success, is much nearer prosperity at thirty-five than twenty-five, and it is therefore wise for these men not to marry in the twenties; but this does not apply to the workingman. In many trades he is laid upon the shelf at thirty-five, and in nearly all trades he receives the largest wages in his life between twenty and thirty. If the young workingman has all his wages to himself, he will probably establish habits of personal comfort, which he cannot keep up when he has to divide with a family — habits which he can, perhaps, never overcome.

The sense of prudence, the necessity for saving, can never come to a primitive, emotional man with the force of a conviction; but the necessity of providing for his children is a powerful incentive. He naturally regards his children as his savings-bank; he expects them to care for him when he gets old, and in some trades old age comes very early. A Jewish tailor was quite lately sent to the Cook County poorhouse, paralyzed beyond recovery at the age of thirty-five. Had his little boy of nine been but a few years older, he might have been spared this sorrow of public charity. He was, in fact, better able to well support a family when he was twenty than when he was thirty-five, for his wages had steadily grown less as the years went on. Another tailor whom I know, who is also a Socialist, always speaks of saving as a bourgeois virtue, one quite impossible to the genuine working-man. He supports a family consisting of himself, a wife and three children, and his two parents on eight dollars a week. He insists it would be criminal not to expend every penny of this amount upon food and shelter, and he expects his children later to care for him.

This economic pressure also accounts for the tendency to put children to work over-young and thus cripple their chances for individual development and usefulness, and with the avaricious parent also leads to exploitation. "I have fed her for fourteen years, now she can help me pay my mortgage" is not an unusual reply when a hard-working father is expostulated with because he would take his bright daughter out of school and put her into a factory.

It has long been a common error for the charity visitor, who is strongly urging her "family" toward self-support, to suggest, or at least connive, that the children be put to work early, although she has not the excuse that the parents have. It is so easy, after one has been taking the industrial view for a long time, to forget the larger and more social claim; to urge that the boy go to work and support his parents, who are receiving charitable aid. She does not realize what a cruel advantage the person who distributes charity has, when she gives advice.

The manager in a huge mercantile establishment employing many children was able to show during a child-labor investigation, that the only children under fourteen years of age in his employ were protégés who had been urged upon him by philanthropic ladies, not only acquaintances of his, but valued patrons of the establishment. It is not that the charity visitor is less wise than other people, but she has fixed her mind so long upon the industrial lameness of her family that she is eager to seize any crutch, however weak, which may enable them to get on.

She has failed to see that the boy who attempts to prematurely support his widowed mother may lower wages, add an illiterate member to the community, and arrest the development of a capable workingman. As she has failed to see that the rules which obtain in regard to the age of marriage in her own family may not apply to the workingman, so also she fails to understand that the present conditions of employment surrounding a factory child are totally unlike those which obtained during the energetic youth of her father.

The child who is prematurely put to work is constantly oppressed by this never ending question of the means of subsistence, and even little children are sometimes almost crushed with the cares of life through their affectionate sympathy. The writer knows a little Italian lad of six to whom the problems of food, clothing, and shelter have become so immediate and pressing that, although an imaginative child, he is unable to see life from any other standpoint. The goblin or bugaboo, feared by the more fortunate child, in his mind, has come to be the need of coal which caused his father hysterical and demonstrative grief when it carried off his mother's inherited linen, the mosaic of St. Joseph, and, worst of all, his own rubber boots. He once came to a party at Hull-House, and was interested in nothing save a gas stove which he saw in the kitchen. He became excited over the discovery that fire could be produced without fuel. "I will tell my father of this stove. You buy no coal, you need only a match. Anybody will give you a match." He was taken to visit at a country-house and at once inquired how much rent was paid for it. On being told carelessly by his hostess that they paid no rent for that house, he came back quite wild with interest that the problem was solved. " Me and my father will go to the country. You get a big house, all warm, without rent." Nothing else in the country interested him but the subject of rent, and he talked of that with an exclusiveness worthy of a single taxer.

The struggle for existence, which is so much harsher among people near the edge of pauperism, sometimes leaves ugly marks on character, and the charity visitor finds these indirect results most mystifying. Parents who work hard and anticipate an old age when they can no longer earn, take care that their children shall expect to divide their wages with them from the very first. Such a parent, when successful, impresses the immature nervous system of the child thus tyrannically establishing habits of obedience, so that the nerves and will may not depart from this control when the child is older. The charity visitor, whose family relation is lifted quite out of this, does not in the least understand the industrial foundation for this family tyranny.

The head of a kindergarten training-class once addressed a club of working women, and spoke of the despotism which is often established over little children. She said that the so-called determination to break a child's will many times arose from a lust of dominion, and she urged the ideal relationship founded upon love and confidence. But many of the women were puzzled. One of them remarked to the writer as she came out of the club room, " If you did not keep control over them from the time they were little, you would never get their wages when they are grown up." Another one said, " Ah, of course she (meaning the speaker) doesn't have to depend upon her children's wages. She can afford to be lax with them,

45

because even if they don't give money to her, she can get along without it."

There are an impressive number of children who uncomplainingly and constantly hand over their weekly wages to their parents, sometimes receiving back ten cents or a quarter for spending-money, but quite as often nothing at all; and the writer knows one girl of twenty-five who for six years has received two cents a week from the constantly falling wages which she earns in a large factory. Is it habit or virtue which holds her steady in this course? If love and tenderness had been substituted for parental despotism, would the mother have had enough affection, enough power of expression to hold her daughter's sense of money obligation through all these years? This girl who spends her paltry two cents on chewing-gum and goes plainly clad in clothes of her mother's choosing, while many of her friends spend their entire wages on those clothes which factory girls love so well, must be held by some powerful force.

The charity visitor finds these subtle and elusive problems most harrowing. The head of a family she is visiting is a man who has become black-listed in a strike. He is not a very good workman, and this, added to his agitator's reputation, keeps him out of work for a long time. The fatal result of being long out of work follows: he becomes less and less eager for it, and gets a "job" less and less frequently. In order to keep up his self-respect, and still more to keep his wife's respect for him, he yields to the little self-deception that this prolonged idleness follows because he was once black-listed, and he gradually becomes a martyr. Deep down in his heart perhaps — but who knows what may be deep down in his heart? Whatever may be in his wife's, she does not show for an instant that she thinks he has grown lazy, and accustomed to see her earn, by sewing and cleaning, most of the scanty income for the family. The charity visitor, however, does see this, and she also sees that the other men who were in the strike have gone back to work. She further knows by inquiry and a little experience that the man is not skilful. She cannot, however, call him lazy and good-for-nothing, and denounce him as worthless as her grandmother might have done, because of certain intellectual conceptions at which she has arrived. She sees other workmen come to him for shrewd advice; she knows that he spends many more hours in the public library reading good books than the average workman has time to do. He has formed no bad habits and has yielded only to those subtle temptations toward a life of leisure which come to the intellectual man. He lacks the qualifications which would induce his union to engage him as a secretary or organizer, but he is a constant speaker at workingmen's meetings, and takes a high moral attitude on the questions discussed there. He contributes a certain intellectuality to his friends, and he has undoubted social value. The neighboring women confide to the charity visitor their

sympathy with his wife, because she has to
work so hard, and because her husband does
not "provide." Their remarks are sharp-
ened by a certain resentment toward the
superiority of the husband's education and
gentle manners. The charity visitor is
ashamed to take this point of view, for she
knows that it is not altogether fair. She is
reminded of a college friend of hers, who
told her that she was not going to allow
her literary husband to write unworthy pot-
boilers for the sake of earning a living. " I
insist that we shall live within my own
income; that he shall not publish until he
is ready, and can give his genuine message."
The charity visitor recalls what she has
heard of another acquaintance, who urged
her husband to decline a lucrative position
as a railroad attorney, because she wished
him to be free to take municipal positions,
and handle public questions without the
inevitable suspicion which unaccountably
attaches itself in a corrupt city to a corpo-
ration attorney. The action of these two

women seemed noble to her, but in their cases they merely lived on a lesser income. In the case of the workingman's wife, she faced living on no income at all, or on the precarious one which she might be able to get together.

She sees that this third woman has made the greatest sacrifice, and she is utterly unwilling to condemn her while praising the friends of her own social position. She realizes, of course, that the situation is changed by the fact that the third family needs charity, while the other two do not; but, after all, they have not asked for it, and their plight was only discovered through an accident to one of the children. The charity visitor has been taught that her mission is to preserve the finest traits to be found in her visited family, and she shrinks from the thought of convincing the wife that her husband is worthless and she suspects that she might turn all this beautiful devotion into complaining drudgery. To be sure, she could give up visiting the family altogether, but she has become much interested in the progress of the crippled child who eagerly anticipates her visits, and she also suspects that she will never know many finer women than the mother. She is unwilling, therefore, to give up the friendship, and goes on bearing her perplexities as best she may.

The first impulse of our charity visitor is to be somewhat severe with her shiftless family for spending money on pleasures and indulging their children out of all proportion to their means. The poor family which receives beans and coal from the county, and pays for a bicycle on the instalment plan, is not unknown to any of us. But as the growth of juvenile crime becomes gradually understood, and as the danger of giving no legitimate and organized pleasure to the child becomes clearer, we remember that primitive man had games long before he cared for a house or regular meals.

There are certain boys in many city neighborhoods who form themselves into little gangs with a leader who is somewhat more intrepid than the rest. Their favorite performance is to break into an untenanted house, to knock off the faucets, and cut the lead pipe, which they sell to the nearest junk dealer. With the money thus procured they buy beer and drink it in little free-booter's groups sitting in the alley. From beginning to end they have the excitement of knowing that they may be seen and caught by the "coppers," and are at times quite breathless with suspense. It is not the least unlike, in motive and execution, the practice of country boys who go forth in squads to set traps for rabbits or to round up a coon.

It is characterized by a pure spirit for adventure, and the vicious training really begins when they are arrested, or when an older boy undertakes to guide them into further excitements. From the very beginning the most enticing and exciting experiences which they have seen have been connected with crime. The policeman embodies all the majesty of successful law and established government in his brass buttons and dazzlingly equipped patrol wagon.

The boy who has been arrested comes back more or less a hero with a tale to tell of the interior recesses of the mysterious police station. The earliest public excitement the child remembers is divided between the rattling fire engines, "the time there was a fire in the next block," and all the tense interest of the patrol wagon "the time the drunkest lady in our street was arrested."

In the first year of their settlement the Hull-House residents took fifty kindergarten children to Lincoln Park, only to be grieved by their apathetic interest in trees and flowers. As they came back with an omnibus full of tired and sleepy children, they were surprised to find them galvanized into sudden life because a patrol wagon rattled by. Their eager little heads popped out of the windows full of questioning: "Was it a man or a woman?" "How many policemen inside?" and eager little tongues began to tell experiences of arrests which baby eyes had witnessed.

The excitement of a chase, the chances of competition, and the love of a fight are all centred in the outward display of crime. The parent who receives charitable aid and yet provides pleasure for his child, and is willing to indulge him in his play, is blindly doing one of the wisest things possible; and no one is more eager for playgrounds and vacation schools than the conscientious charity visitor.

This very imaginative impulse and attempt to live in a pictured world of their own, which seems the simplest prerogative of childhood, often leads the boys into difficulty. Three boys aged seven, nine, and ten were once brought into a neighboring police station under the charge of pilfering and destroying property. They had dug a cave under a railroad viaduct in which they had spent many days and nights of the summer vacation. They had "swiped" potatoes and other vegetables from hucksters' carts, which they had cooked and eaten in true brigand fashion; they had decorated the interior of the excavation with stolen junk, representing swords and firearms, to their romantic imaginations. The father of the ringleader was a janitor living in a building five miles away in a prosperous portion of the city. The landlord did not want an active boy in the building, and his mother was dead; the janitor paid for the boy's board and lodging to a needy woman living near the viaduct. She conscientiously gave him his breakfast and supper, and left something in the house for his dinner every morning when she went to work in a neighboring factory; but was too tired by night to challenge his statement that he "would rather sleep outdoors in the summer," or to investigate what he did during the day. In the meantime the three boys lived in a world of their own, made up from the reading of adventurous stories and their vivid imaginations, steadily pilfering more and more as the days went by, and actually imperilling the safety of the traffic passing over the street on the top of the viaduct. In spite of vigorous exertions on their behalf, one of the boys was sent to the Reform School, comforting himself with the conclusive remark, " Well, we had fun anyway, and maybe they will let us dig a cave at the School; it is in the country, where we can't hurt anything."

In addition to books of adventure, or even reading of any sort, the scenes and ideals of the theatre largely form the manners and morals of the young people. " Going to the theatre " is indeed the most common and satisfactory form of recreation. Many boys who conscientiously give all their wages to their mothers have returned each week ten cents to pay for a seat in the gallery of a theatre on Sunday afternoon. It is their one satisfactory glimpse of life — the moment when they "issue forth from themselves" and are stirred and thoroughly interested. They quite simply adopt as their own, and imitate as best they can, all that they see there. In moments of genuine grief and excitement the words and the gestures they employ are those copied from the stage, and the tawdry expression often conflicts hideously with the fine and genuine emotion of which it is the inadequate and vulgar vehicle.

As in the matter of dress, more refined and simpler manners and mode of expressions are unseen by them, and they must perforce copy what they know.

If we agree with a recent definition of Art, as that which causes the spectator to lose his sense of isolation, there is no doubt that the popular theatre, with all its faults, more nearly fulfils the function of art for the multitude of working people than all the "free galleries" and picture exhibits combined.

The greatest difficulty is experienced when the two standards come sharply together, and when both sides make an attempt at understanding and explanation. The difficulty of making clear one's own ethical standpoint is at times insurmountable. A woman who had bought and sold school books stolen from the school fund, — books which are all plainly marked with a red stamp, — came to Hull House one morning in great distress because she had been arrested, and begged a resident "to speak to the judge." She gave as a reason the fact that the House had known her for six years, and had once been very good to her when her little girl was buried. The resident more than suspected that her visitor knew the school books were stolen when buying them, and any attempt to talk upon that subject was evidently considered very rude. The visitor wished to get out of her trial, and evidently saw no reason why the House should not help her. The alderman was out of town, so she could not go to him. After a long conversation the visitor entirely failed to get another point of view and went away grieved and disappointed at a refusal, thinking the resident simply disobliging; wondering, no doubt, why such a mean woman had once been good to her; leaving the resident, on the other hand, utterly baffled and in the state of mind she would have been in, had she brutally insisted that a little child should lift weights too heavy for its undeveloped muscles.

Such a situation brings out the impossibility of substituting a higher ethical standard for a lower one without similarity of experience, but it is not as painful as that illustrated by the following example, in which the highest ethical standard yet attained by the charity recipient is broken down, and the substituted one not in the least understood : —

A certain charity visitor is peculiarly appealed to by the weakness and pathos of forlorn old age. She is responsible for the

well-being of perhaps a dozen old women to
whom she sustains a sincerely affectionate
and almost filial relation. Some of them
learn to take her benefactions quite as if
they came from their own relatives, grum-
bling at all she does, and scolding her with
a family freedom. One of these poor old
women was injured in a fire years ago.
She has but the fragment of a hand left, and
is grievously crippled in her feet. Through
years of pain she had become addicted to
opium, and when she first came under the
visitor's care, was only held from the poorhouse by the awful thought that she would
there perish without her drug. Five years
of tender care have done wonders for her.
She lives in two neat little rooms, where
with her thumb and two fingers she makes
innumerable quilts, which she sells and gives
away with the greatest delight. Her opium
is regulated to a set amount taken each day,
and she has been drawn away from much
drinking. She is a voracious reader, and has
her head full of strange tales made up from

books and her own imagination. At one time it seemed impossible to do anything for her in Chicago, and she was kept for two years in a suburb, where the family of the charity visitor lived, and where she was nursed through several hazardous illnesses. She now lives a better life than she did, but she is still far from being a model old woman. The neighbors are constantly shocked by the fact that she is supported and comforted by a " charity lady," while at the same time she occasionally "rushes the growler," scolding at the boys lest they jar her in her tottering walk. The care of her has broken through even that second standard, which the neighborhood had learned to recognize as the standard of charitable societies, that only the " worthy poor " are to be helped ; that temperance and thrift are the virtues which receive the plums of benevolence. The old lady herself is conscious of this criticism. Indeed, irate neighbors tell her to her face that she doesn't in the least deserve what she gets. In order to

disarm them, and at the same time to ex-
plain what would otherwise seem loving-
kindness so colossal as to be abnormal, she
tells them that during her sojourn in the
suburb she discovered an awful family
secret, — a horrible scandal connected with
the long-suffering charity visitor; that it is
in order to prevent the divulgence of this
that she constantly receives her ministrations.   Some of her perplexed neighbors
accept this explanation as simple and offering a solution of this vexed problem. Doubtless many of them have a glimpse of the
real state of affairs, of the love and patience
which ministers to need irrespective of
worth.   But the standard is too high for
most of them, and it sometimes seems unfortunate to break down the second standard, which holds that people who " rush the
growler " are not worthy of charity, and that
there is a certain justice attained when they
go to the poorhouse. It is certainly dangerous to break down the lower, unless the
higher is made clear.

Just when our affection becomes large enough to care for the unworthy among the poor as we would care for the unworthy among our own kin, is certainly a perplexing question. To say that it should never be so, is a comment upon our democratic relations to them which few of us would be willing to make.

Of what use is all this striving and perplexity? Has the experience any value? It is certainly genuine, for it induces an occasional charity visitor to live in a tenement house as simply as the other tenants do. It drives others to give up visiting the poor altogether, because, they claim, it is quite impossible unless the individual becomes a member of a sisterhood, which requires, as some of the Roman Catholic sisterhoods do, that the member first take the vows of obedience and poverty, so that she can have nothing to give save as it is first given to her, and thus she is not harassed by a constant attempt at adjustment.

Both the tenement-house resident and the sister assume to have put themselves upon the industrial level of their neighbors, although they have left out the most awful element of poverty, that of imminent fear of starvation and a neglected old age.

The young charity visitor who goes from a family living upon a most precarious industrial level to her own home in a prosperous part of the city, if she is sensitive at all, is never free from perplexities which our growing democracy forces upon her.

We sometimes say that our charity is too scientific, but we would doubtless be much more correct in our estimate if we said that it is not scientific enough. We dislike the entire arrangement of cards alphabetically classified according to streets and names of families, with the unrelated and meaningless details attached to them. Our feeling of revolt is probably not unlike that which afflicted the students of botany and geology in the middle of the last century, when flowers were tabulated in alphabetical order,

64

when geology was taught by colored charts and thin books. No doubt the students, wearied to death, many times said that it was all too scientific, and were much perplexed and worried when they found traces of structure and physiology which their so-called scientific principles were totally unable to account for. But all this happened before science had become evolutionary and scientific at all, before it had a principle of life from within. The very indications and discoveries which formerly perplexed, later illumined and made the study absorbing and vital.

We are singularly slow to apply this evolutionary principle to human affairs in general, although it is fast being applied to the education of children. We are at last learning to follow the development of the child; to expect certain traits under certain conditions; to adapt methods and matter to his growing mind. No "advanced educator" can allow himself to be so absorbed in the question of what a child

ought to be as to exclude the discovery of
what he is. But in our charitable efforts
we think much more of what a man ought
to be than of what he is or of what he may
become; and we ruthlessly force our conventions and standards upon him, with a
sternness which we would consider stupid
indeed did an educator use it in forcing his
mature intellectual convictions upon an undeveloped mind.

Let us take the example of a timid child,
who cries when he is put to bed because
he is afraid of the dark. The "soft-hearted"
parent stays with him, simply because he is
sorry for him and wants to comfort him.
The scientifically trained parent stays with
him, because he realizes that the child is in
a stage of development in which his imagination has the best of him, and in which
it is impossible to reason him out of a belief
in ghosts. These two parents, wide apart
in point of view, after all act much alike,
and both very differently from the pseudo-
scientific parent, who acts from dogmatic

conviction and is sure he is right. He
talks of developing his child's self-respect
and good sense, and leaves him to cry himself to sleep, demanding powers of self-
control and development which the child
does not possess. There is no doubt that
our development of charity methods has
reached this pseudo-scientific and stilted
stage. We have learned to condemn un-
thinking, ill-regulated kind-heartedness, and
we take great pride in mere repression much
as the stern parent tells the visitor below
how admirably he is rearing the child, who
is hysterically crying upstairs and laying
the foundation for future nervous disorders.
The pseudo-scientific spirit, or rather, the
undeveloped stage of our philanthropy, is
perhaps most clearly revealed in our tendency to lay constant stress on negative
action. " Don't give ; " "don't break down
self-respect," we are constantly told. We
distrust the human impulse as well as the
teachings of our own experience, and in
their stead substitute dogmatic rules for

conduct. We forget that the accumulation of knowledge and the holding of convictions must finally result in the application of that knowledge and those convictions to life itself; that the necessity for activity and a pull upon the sympathies is so severe, that all the knowledge in the possession of the visitor is constantly applied, and she has a reasonable chance for an ultimate intellectual comprehension. Indeed, part of the perplexity in the administration of charity comes from the fact that the type of person drawn to it is the one who insists that her convictions shall not be unrelated to action. Her moral concepts constantly tend to float away from her, unless they have a basis in the concrete relation of life. She is confronted with the task of reducing her scruples to action, and of converging many wills, so as to unite the strength of all of them into one accomplishment, the value of which no one can foresee.

On the other hand, the young woman who has succeeded in expressing her social compunction through charitable effort finds that the wider social activity, and the contact with the larger experience, not only increases her sense of social obligation but at the same time recasts her social ideals. She is chagrined to discover that in the actual task of reducing her social scruples to action, her humble beneficiaries are far in advance of her, not in charity or singleness of purpose, but in self-sacrificing action. She reaches the old-time virtue of humility by a social process, not in the old way, as the man who sits by the side of the road and puts dust upon his head, calling himself a contrite sinner, but she gets the dust upon her head because she has stumbled and fallen in the road through her efforts to push forward the mass, to march with her fellows. She has socialized her virtues not only through a social aim but by a social process.

The Hebrew prophet made three requirements from those who would join the great forward-moving procession led by Jehovah. " To love mercy " and at the same time " to do justly " is the difficult task; to fulfil the first requirement alone is to fall into the error of indiscriminate giving with all its disastrous results; to fulfil the second solely is to obtain the stern policy of withholding, and it results in such a dreary lack of sympathy and understanding that the establishment of justice is impossible. It may be that the combination of the two can never be attained save as we fulfil still the third requirement — " to walk humbly with God," which may mean to walk for many dreary miles beside the lowliest of His creatures, not even in that peace of mind which the company of the humble is popularly supposed to afford, but rather with the pangs and throes to which the poor human understanding is subjected whenever it attempts to comprehend the meaning of life.

CHAPTER III

FILIAL RELATIONS

THERE are many people in every community who have not felt the "social compunction," who do not share the effort toward a higher social morality, who are even unable to sympathetically interpret it. Some of these have been shielded from the inevitable and salutary failures which the trial of new powers involve, because they are content to attain standards of virtue demanded by an easy public opinion, and others of them have exhausted their moral energy in attaining to the current standard of individual and family righteousness.

Such people, who form the bulk of contented society, demand that the radical, the reformer, shall be without stain or question in his personal and family relations, and judge most harshly any deviation from the established standards. There is a certain justice in this: it expresses the inherent conservatism of the mass of men, that none of the established virtues which have been so slowly and hardly acquired shall be sacrificed for the sake of making problematic advance; that the individual, in his attempt to develop and use the new and exalted virtue, shall not fall into the easy temptation of letting the ordinary ones slip through his fingers.

This instinct to conserve the old standards, combined with a distrust of the new standard, is a constant difficulty in the way of those experiments and advances depending upon the initiative of women, both because women are the more sensitive to the individual and family claims, and because their training has tended to make them content with the response to these claims alone.

There is no doubt that, in the effort to sustain the moral energy necessary to work out a more satisfactory social relation, the individual often sacrifices the energy which should legitimately go into the fulfilment of personal and family claims, to what he considers the higher claim.

In considering the changes which our increasing democracy is constantly making upon various relationships, it is impossible to ignore the filial relation. This chapter deals with the relation between parents and their grown-up daughters, as affording an explicit illustration of the perplexity and mal-adjustment brought about by the various attempts of young women to secure a more active share in the community life. We constantly see parents very much disconcerted and perplexed in regard to their daughters when these daughters undertake work lying quite outside of traditional and family interests. These parents insist that the girl is carried away by a foolish enthusiasm, that she is in search of a career, that she is restless and does not know what she wants. They will give any reason, almost, rather than the recognition of a genuine and dignified claim. Possibly all this is due to the fact that for so many hundreds of years women have had no larger interests, no participation in the affairs lying quite outside personal and family claims. Any attempt that the individual woman formerly made to subordinate or renounce the family claim was inevitably construed to mean that she was setting up her own will against that of her family's for selfish ends. It was concluded that she could have no motive larger than a desire to serve her family, and her attempt to break away must therefore be wilful and self-indulgent.

The family logically consented to give her up at her marriage, when she was enlarging the family tie by founding another family. It was easy to understand that they permitted and even promoted her going to college, travelling in Europe, or any other means of self-improvement, because these merely meant the development and cultivation of one of its own members. When, however, she responded to her impulse to fulfil the social or democratic claim, she violated every tradition.

The mind of each one of us reaches back to our first struggles as we emerged from self-willed childhood into a recognition of family obligations. We have all gradually learned to respond to them, and yet most of us have had at least fleeting glimpses of what it might be to disregard them and the elemental claim they make upon us. We have yielded at times to the temptation of ignoring them for selfish aims, of considering the individual and not the family convenience, and we remember with shame the self-pity which inevitably followed. But just as we have learned to adjust the personal and family claims, and to find an orderly development impossible without recognition of both, so perhaps we are called upon now to make a second adjustment between the family and the social claim, in which neither shall lose and both be ennobled.

The attempt to bring about a healing

compromise in which the two shall be ad·
justed in proper relation is not an easy one.
It is difficult to distinguish between the
outward act of him who in following one
legitimate claim has been led into the tem·
porary violation of another, and the outward
act of him who deliberately renounces a just
claim and throws aside all obligation for the
sake of his own selfish and individual development. The man, for instance, who deserts
his family that he may cultivate an artistic
sensibility, or acquire what he considers
more fulness of life for himself, must always
arouse our contempt. Breaking the marriage tie as Ibsen's "Nora" did, to obtain
a larger self-development, or holding to it
as George Eliot's "Romola" did, because
of the larger claim of the state and society,
must always remain two distinct paths. The
collision of interests, each of which has a
real moral basis and a right to its own place
in life, is bound to be more or less tragic.
It is the struggle between two claims, the
destruction of either of which would bring

ruin to the ethical life. Curiously enough, it is almost exactly this contradiction which is the tragedy set forth by the Greek dramatist, who asserted that the gods who watch over the sanctity of the family bond must yield to the higher claims of the gods of the state. The failure to recognize the social claim as legitimate causes the trouble; the suspicion constantly remains that woman's public efforts are merely selfish and captious, and are not directed to the general good. This suspicion will never be dissipated until parents, as well as daughters, feel the democratic impulse and recognize the social claim.

Our democracy is making inroads upon the family, the oldest of human institutions, and a claim is being advanced which in a certain sense is larger than the family claim. The claim of the state in time of war has long been recognized, so that in its name the family has given up sons and husbands and even the fathers of little children. If we can once see the claims of society in any such light, if its misery and need can be made clear and urged as an explicit claim, as the state urges its claims in the time of danger, then for the first time the daughter who desires to minister to that need will be recognized as acting conscientiously. This recognition may easily come first through the emotions, and may be admitted as a response to pity and mercy long before it is formulated and perceived by the intellect.

The family as well as the state we are all called upon to maintain as the highest institutions which the race has evolved for its safeguard and protection. But merely to preserve these institutions is not enough. There come periods of reconstruction, during which the task is laid upon a passing generation, to enlarge the function and carry forward the ideal of a long-established institution. There is no doubt that many women, consciously and unconsciously, are struggling with this task. The family, like every other element of human life, is susceptible of progress, and from epoch to epoch its tendencies and aspirations are enlarged, although its duties can never be abrogated and its obligations can never be cancelled. It is impossible to bring about the higher development by any self-assertion or breaking away of the individual will. The new growth in the plant swelling against the sheath, which at the same time imprisons and protects it, must still be the truest type of progress. The family in its entirety must be carried out into the larger life. Its various members together must recognize and acknowledge the validity of the social obligation. When this does not occur we have a most flagrant example of the ill-adjustment and misery arising when an ethical code is applied too rigorously and too conscientiously to conditions which are no longer the same as when the code was instituted, and for which it was never designed. We have all seen parental control and the family claim assert their authority in fields of effort which belong to the adult judgment of the child and

pertain to activity quite outside the family
life. Probably the distinctively family
tragedy of which we all catch glimpses
now and then, is the assertion of this authority through all the entanglements of
wounded affection and misunderstanding.
We see parents and children acting from
conscientious motives and with the tenderest affection, yet bringing about a misery
which can scarcely be hidden.

Such glimpses remind us of that tragedy
enacted centuries ago in Assisi, when the
eager young noble cast his very clothing
at his father's feet, dramatically renouncing
his filial allegiance, and formally subjecting
the narrow family claim to the wider and
more universal duty. All the conflict of
tragedy ensued which might have been
averted, had the father recognized the
higher claim, and had he been willing to
subordinate and adjust his own claim to
it. The father considered his son disre-
spectful and hard-hearted, yet we know St.
Francis to have been the most tender and

loving of men, responsive to all possible
ties, even to those of inanimate nature.
We know that by his affections he freed
the frozen life of his time. The elements
of tragedy lay in the narrowness of the
father's mind; in his lack of comprehension and his lack of sympathy with the
power which was moving his son, and
which was but part of the religious revival
which swept Europe from end to end in
the early part of the thirteenth century;
the same power which built the cathe-
drals of the North, and produced the saints
and sages of the South. But the father's
situation was nevertheless genuine; he felt
his heart sore and angry, and his dignity
covered with disrespect. He could not,
indeed, have felt otherwise, unless he had
been touched by the fire of the same revival, and lifted out of and away from the
contemplation of himself and his narrower
claim. It is another proof that the notion of a larger obligation can only come
through the response to an enlarged inter-

est in life and in the social movements around us.

The grown-up son has so long been considered a citizen with well-defined duties and a need of "making his way in the world," that the family claim is urged much less strenuously in his case, and as a matter of authority, it ceases gradually to be made at all. In the case of the grown-up daughter, however, who is under no necessity of earning a living, and who has no strong artistic bent, taking her to Paris to study painting or to Germany to study music, the years immediately following her graduation from college are too often filled with a restlessness and unhappiness which might be avoided by a little clear thinking, and by an adaptation of our code of family ethics to modern conditions. It is always difficult for the family to regard the daughter otherwise than as a family possession. From her babyhood she has been the charm and grace of the household, and it is hard to think of her

as an integral part of the social order,
hard to believe that she has duties outside of the family, to the state and to
society in the larger sense. This assumption that the daughter is solely an inspiration and refinement to the family itself and
its own immediate circle, that her delicacy
and polish are but outward symbols of her
father's protection and prosperity, worked
very smoothly for the most part so long
as her education was in line with it. When
there was absolutely no recognition of the
entity of woman's life beyond the family,
when the outside claims upon her were
still wholly unrecognized, the situation was
simple, and the finishing school harmoni-
ously and elegantly answered all requirements. She was fitted to grace the fireside
and to add lustre to that social circle which
her parents selected for her. But this family
assumption has been notably broken into,
and educational ideas no longer fit it. Modern education recognizes woman quite apart
from family or society claims, and gives

DEMOCRACY AND SOCIAL ETHICS

her the training which for many years has
been deemed successful for highly developing a man's individuality and freeing his
powers for independent action. Perplexities often occur when the daughter returns
from college and finds that this recognition has been but partially accomplished.
When she attempts to act upon the assumption of its accomplishment, she finds
herself jarring upon ideals which are so
entwined with filial piety, so rooted in the
tenderest affections of which the human
heart is capable, that both daughter and
parents are shocked and startled when they
discover what is happening, and they
scarcely venture to analyze the situation.
The ideal for the education of woman has
changed under the pressure of a new claim.
The family has responded to the extent of
granting the education, but they are jeal-
ous of the new claim and assert the family
claim as over against it.

The modern woman finds herself educated to recognize a stress of social obliga-

tion which her family did not in the least
anticipate when they sent her to college.
She finds herself, in addition, under an
impulse to act her part as a citizen of the
world. She accepts her family inheritance
with loyalty and affection, but she has entered into a wider inheritance as well,
which, for lack of a better phrase, we call
the social claim. This claim has been recognized for four years in her training, but
after her return from college the family
claim is again exclusively and strenuously
asserted. The situation has all the discomfort of transition and compromise.
The daughter finds a constant and totally
unnecessary conflict between the social and
the family claims. In most cases the
former is repressed and gives way to the
family claim, because the latter is concrete
and definitely asserted, while the social
demand is vague and unformulated. In
such instances the girl quietly submits, but
she feels wronged whenever she allows her
mind to dwell upon the situation. She

either hides her hurt, and splendid reserves of enthusiasm and capacity go to waste, or her zeal and emotions are turned inward, and the result is an unhappy woman, whose heart is consumed by vain regrets and desires.

If the college woman is not thus quietly reabsorbed, she is even reproached for her discontent. She is told to be devoted to her family, inspiring and responsive to her social circle, and to give the rest of her time to further self-improvement and enjoyment. She expects to do this, and responds to these claims to the best of her ability, even heroically sometimes. But where is the larger life of which she has dreamed so long? That life which surrounds and completes the individual and family life? She has been taught that it is her duty to share this life, and her highest privilege to extend it. This divergence between her self-centred existence and her best convictions becomes constantly more apparent. But the situation is not even so simple as a conflict between her affections and her intellectual convictions, although even that is tumultuous enough, also the emotional nature is divided against itself. The social claim is a demand upon the emotions as well as upon the intellect, and in ignoring it she represses not only her convictions but lowers her springs of vitality. Her life is full of contradictions. She looks out into the world, longing that some demand be made upon her powers, for they are too untrained to furnish an initiative. When her health gives way under this strain, as it often does, her physician invariably advises a rest. But to be put to bed and fed on milk is not what she requires. What she needs is simple, health-giving activity, which, involving the use of all her faculties, shall be a response to all the claims which she so keenly feels.

It is quite true that the family often resents her first attempts to be part of a life quite outside their own, because the college woman frequently makes these first attempts most awkwardly; her faculties have not been trained in the line of action. She lacks the ability to apply her knowledge and theories to life itself and to its complicated situations. This is largely the fault of her training and of the one-sidedness of educational methods. The colleges have long been full of the best ethical teaching, insisting that the good of the whole must ultimately be the measure of effort, and that the individual can only secure his own rights as he labors to secure those of others. But while the teaching has included an ever-broadening range of obligation and has insisted upon the recognition of the claims of human brotherhood, the training has been singularly individualistic; it has fostered ambitions for personal distinction, and has trained the faculties almost exclusively in the direction of intellectual accumulation. Doubtless, woman's education is at fault, in that it has failed to recognize certain needs, and has failed to cultivate and

guide the larger desires of which all generous young hearts are full.

During the most formative years of life,
it gives the young girl no contact with the
feebleness of childhood, the pathos of suffering, or the needs of old age. It gathers
together crude youth in contact only with
each other and with mature men and women
who are there for the purpose of their mental direction. The tenderest promptings
are bidden to bide their time. This could
only be justifiable if a definite outlet were
provided when they leave college. Doubtless the need does not differ widely in men
and women, but women not absorbed in professional or business life, in the years immediately following college, are baldly brought
face to face with the deficiencies of their
training. Apparently every obstacle is removed, and the college woman is at last
free to begin the active life, for which, during so many years, she has been preparing.
But during this so-called preparation, her
faculties have been trained solely for ac-

cumulation, and she has learned to utterly distrust the finer impulses of her nature, which would naturally have connected her with human interests outside of her family and her own immediate social circle. All through school and college the young soul dreamed of self-sacrifice, of succor to the helpless and of tenderness to the unfortunate. We persistently distrust these desires, and, unless they follow well-defined lines, we repress them with every device of convention and caution.

One summer the writer went from a two weeks' residence in East London, where she had become sick and bewildered by the sights and sounds encountered there, directly to Switzerland. She found the beaten routes of travel filled with young English men and women who could walk many miles a day, and who could climb peaks so inaccessible that the feats received honorable mention in Alpine journals, — a result which filled their families with joy and pride. These young people knew to a nicety the proper diet and clothing which would best contribute toward endurance. Everything was very fine about them save their motive power. The writer does not refer to the hard-worked men and women who were taking a vacation, but to the leisured young people, to whom this period was the most serious of the year, and filled with the most strenuous exertion. They did not, of course, thoroughly enjoy it, for we are too complicated to be content with mere exercise. Civilization has bound us too closely with our brethren for any one of us to be long happy in the cultivation of mere individual force or in the accumulation of mere muscular energy.

With Whitechapel constantly in mind, it was difficult not to advise these young people to use some of this muscular energy of which they were so proud, in cleaning neglected alleys and paving soggy streets. Their stores of enthusiasm might stir to energy the listless men and women of East London and utilize latent social forces. The exercise would be quite as good, the need of endurance as great, the care for proper dress and food as important; but the motives for action would be turned from selfish ones into social ones. Such an appeal would doubtless be met with a certain response from the young people, but would never be countenanced by their families for an instant.

Fortunately a beginning has been made in another direction, and a few parents have already begun to consider even their little children in relation to society as well as to the family. The young mothers who attend "Child Study" classes have a larger notion of parenthood and expect given characteristics from their children, at certain ages and under certain conditions. They quite calmly watch the various attempts of a child to assert his individuality, which so often takes the form of opposition to the wishes of the family and to the rule of the household. They recognize as acting under the same law of development the little child of three who persistently runs away and pretends not to hear his mother's voice, the boy of ten who violently, although temporarily, resents control of any sort, and the grown-up son who, by an individualized and trained personality, is drawn into pursuits and interests quite alien to those of his family.

This attempt to take the parental relation somewhat away from mere personal experience, as well as the increasing tendency of parents to share their children's pursuits and interests, will doubtless finally result in a better understanding of the social obligation. The understanding, which results from identity of interests, would seem to confirm the conviction that in the complicated life of to-day there is no education so admirable as that education which comes from participation in the constant trend of events. There is no doubt that most of the misunderstandings of life are due to partial intelligence, because our experiences have been so unlike that we cannot comprehend each other. The old difficulties incident to the clash of two codes of morals must drop away, as the experiences of various members of the family become larger and more identical.

At the present moment, however, many of those difficulties still exist and may be seen all about us. In order to illustrate the situation baldly, and at the same time to put it dramatically, it may be well to take an instance concerning which we have no personal feeling. The tragedy of King Lear has been selected, although we have been accustomed so long to give him our sympathy as the victim of the ingratitude of his two older daughters, and of the apparent coldness of Cordelia, that we have not sufficiently considered the weakness of his fatherhood, revealed by the fact that he should get himself into so entangled and unhappy a relation to all of his children. In our pity for Lear, we fail to analyze his character. The King on his throne exhibits utter lack of self-control. The King in the storm gives way

to the same emotion, in repining over
the wickedness of his children, which he
formerly exhibited in his indulgent treatment of them.

It might be illuminating to discover
wherein he had failed, and why his old
age found him roofless in spite of the fact
that he strenuously urged the family claim
with his whole conscience. At the open-
ing of the drama he sat upon his throne,
ready for the enjoyment which an indulgent parent expects when he has given
gifts to his children. From the two elder,
the responses for the division of his lands
were graceful and fitting, but he longed
to hear what Cordelia, his youngest and
best beloved child, would say. He looked
toward her expectantly, but instead of
delight and gratitude there was the first
dawn of character. Cordelia made the
awkward attempt of an untrained soul to
be honest and scrupulously to express
her inmost feeling. The king was baffled
and distressed by this attempt at self-

expression. It was new to him that his daughter should be moved by a principle obtained outside himself, which even his imagination could not follow; that she had caught the notion of an existence in which her relation as a daughter played but a part. She was transformed by a dignity which recast her speech and made it self-contained. She found herself in the sweep of a feeling so large that the immediate loss of a kingdom seemed of little consequence to her. Even an act which might be construed as disrespect to her father was justified in her eyes, because she was vainly striving to fill out this larger conception of duty. The test which comes sooner or later to many parents had come to Lear, to maintain the tenderness of the relation between father and child, after that relation had become one between adults, to be content with the responses made by the adult child to the family claim, while at the same time she responded to the claims of the rest of life. The mind of Lear was not big enough for this test; he failed to see anything but the personal slight involved, and the ingratitude alone reached him. It was impossible for him to calmly watch his child developing beyond the stretch of his own mind and sympathy.

That a man should be so absorbed in his own indignation as to fail to apprehend his child's thought, that he should lose his affection in his anger, simply reveals the fact that his own emotions are dearer to him than his sense of paternal obligation. Lear apparently also ignored the common ancestry of Cordelia and himself, and forgot her royal inheritance of magnanimity. He had thought of himself so long as a noble and indulgent father that he had lost the faculty by which he might perceive himself in the wrong. Even in the midst of the storm he declared himself more sinned against than sinning. He could believe any amount of kindness and goodness of himself, but could imagine no fidelity on the part of Cordelia unless she gave him the sign he demanded.

At length he suffered many hardships; his spirit was buffeted and broken; he lost his reason as well as his kingdom; but for the first time his experience was identical with the experience of the men around him, and he came to a larger conception of life. He put himself in the place of "the poor naked wretches," and unexpectedly found healing and comfort. He took poor Tim in his arms from a sheer desire for human contact and animal warmth, a primitive and genuine need, through which he suddenly had a view of the world which he had never had from his throne, and from this moment his heart began to turn toward Cordelia.

In reading the tragedy of King Lear, Cordelia receives a full share of our censure. Her first words are cold, and we are shocked by her lack of tenderness. Why should she ignore her father's need for indulgence, and be unwilling to give him what he so obviously craved? We see in the old king "the over-mastering desire of being beloved, selfish, and yet characteristic of the selfishness of a loving and kindly nature alone." His eagerness produces in us a strange pity for him, and we are impatient that his youngest and best-beloved child cannot feel this, even in the midst of her search for truth and her newly acquired sense of a higher duty. It seems to us a narrow conception that would break thus abruptly with the past and would assume that her father had no part in the new life. We want to remind her "that pity, memory, and faithfulness are natural ties," and surely as much to be prized as is the development of her own soul. We do not admire the Cordelia who through her self-absorption deserts her father, as we later admire the same woman who comes back from France that she may include her father in her happiness and freer life. The first had selfishly taken her salvation for herself alone, and it was not until her conscience had de-

veloped in her new life that she was driven
back to her father, where she perished,
drawn into the cruelty and wrath which
had now become objective and tragic.

Historically considered, the relation of
Lear to his children was archaic and bar-
baric, indicating merely the beginning of
a family life since developed. His paternal
expression was one of domination and indulgence, without the perception of the needs
of his children, without any anticipation of
their entrance into a wider life, or any belief
that they could have a worthy life apart
from him. If that rudimentary conception
of family life ended in such violent disaster,
the fact that we have learned to be more
decorous in our conduct does not demon-
strate that by following the same line of
theory we may not reach a like misery.

Wounded affection there is sure to be,
but this could be reduced to a modicum if
we could preserve a sense of the relation of
the individual to the family, and of the latter
to society, and if we had been given a code

of ethics dealing with these larger relationships, instead of a code designed to apply so exclusively to relationships obtaining only between individuals.

Doubtless the clashes and jars which we all feel most keenly are those which occur when two standards of morals, both honestly held and believed in, are brought sharply together. The awkwardness and constraint we experience when two standards of conventions and manners clash but feebly prefigure this deeper difference.

CHAPTER IV

HOUSEHOLD ADJUSTMENT

IF we could only be judged or judge other people by purity of motive, life would be much simplified, but that would be to abandon the contention made in the first chapter, that the processes of life are as important as its aims. We can all recall acquaintances of whose integrity of purpose we can have no doubt, but who cause much confusion as they proceed to the accomplishment of that purpose, who indeed are often insensible to their own mistakes and harsh in their judgments of other people because they are so confident of their own inner integrity.

This tendency to be so sure of integrity of purpose as to be unsympathetic and hardened to the means by which it is accomplished, is perhaps nowhere so obvious as in the household itself. It nowhere operates as so constant a force as in the minds of the women who in all the perplexity of industrial transition are striving to administer domestic affairs. The ethics held by them are for the most part the individual and family codes, untouched by the larger social conceptions.

These women, rightly confident of their household and family integrity and holding to their own code of morals, fail to see the household in its social aspect. Possibly no relation has been so slow to respond to the social ethics which we are now considering, as that between the household employer and the household employee, or, as it is still sometimes called, that between mistress and servant.

This persistence of the individual code in relation to the household may be partly accounted for by the fact that orderly life and, in a sense, civilization itself, grew from the concentration of interest in one place, and that moral feeling first became centred in a limited number of persons. From the

familiar proposition that the home began because the mother was obliged to stay in one
spot in order to cherish the child, we can see
a foundation for the belief that if women are
much away from home, the home itself will be
destroyed and all ethical progress endangered.

We have further been told that the earliest dances and social gatherings were most
questionable in their purposes, and that it
was, therefore, the good and virtuous women
who first stayed at home, until gradually the
two — the woman who stayed at home and
the woman who guarded her virtue — became
synonymous. A code of ethics was thus
developed in regard to woman's conduct,
and her duties were logically and carefully
limited to her own family circle. When it
became impossible to adequately minister to
the needs of this circle without the help of
many people who did not strictly belong to
the family, although they were part of the
household, they were added as aids merely
for supplying these needs. When women
were the brewers and bakers, the fullers,

dyers, spinners, and weavers, the soap and
candle makers, they administered large in-
dustries, but solely from the family point
of view. Only a few hundred years ago,
woman had complete control of the manufacturing of many commodities which now
figure so largely in commerce, and it is evident that she let the manufacturing of these
commodities go into the hands of men, as
soon as organization and a larger conception of their production were required. She
felt no responsibility for their management
when they were taken from the home to the
factory, for deeper than her instinct to manufacture food and clothing for her family was
her instinct to stay with them, and by isolation and care to guard them from evil.

She had become convinced that a woman's
duty extended only to her own family, and
that the world outside had no claim upon
her. The British matron ordered her
maidens aright, when they were spinning
under her own roof, but she felt no compunction of conscience when the morals

and health of young girls were endangered in the overcrowded and insanitary factories. The code of family ethics was established in her mind so firmly that it excluded any notion of social effort.

It is quite possible to accept this explanation of the origin of morals, and to believe that the preservation of the home is at the foundation of all that is best in civilization, without at the same time insisting that the separate preparation and serving of food is an inherent part of the structure and sanctity of the home, or that those who minister to one household shall minister to that exclusively. But to make this distinction seems difficult, and almost invariably the sense of obligation to the family becomes confused with a certain sort of domestic management. The moral issue involved in one has become inextricably combined with the industrial difficulty involved in the other, and it is at this point that so many perplexed housekeepers, through the confusion of the two problems, take a difficult and untenable position.

There are economic as well as ethical reasons for this survival of a simpler code. The wife of a workingman still has a distinct economic value to her husband. She cooks, cleans, washes, and mends — services for which, before his marriage, he paid ready money. The wife of the successful business or professional man does not do this. He continues to pay for his cooking, house service, and washing. The mending, however, is still largely performed by his wife; indeed, the stockings are pathetically retained and their darning given an exaggerated importance, as if women instinctively felt that these mended stockings were the last remnant of the entire household industry, of which they were formerly mistresses. But one industry, the cooking and serving of foods to her own family, woman has never relinquished. It has, therefore, never been organized, either by men or women, and is in an undeveloped state. Each employer of household labor views it solely from the family standpoint. The ethics prevailing in regard to it are distinctly personal and unsocial, and result in the unique isolation of the household employee.

As industrial conditions have changed, the household has simplified, from the mediæval affair of journeymen, apprentices, and maidens who spun and brewed to the family proper; to those who love each other and live together in ties of affection and consanguinity. Were this process complete, we should have no problem of household employment. But, even in households comparatively humble, there is still one alien, one who is neither loved nor loving.

The modern family has dropped the man who made its shoes, the woman who spun its clothes, and, to a large extent, the woman who washes them, but it stoutly refuses to drop the woman who cooks its food and ministers directly to its individual comfort; it strangely insists that to do that would be to destroy the family life itself. The cook is uncomfortable, the family is uncomfortable; but it will not drop her as all her fellow-workers have been dropped, although the cook herself insists upon it. So far has this insistence gone that every possible concession is made to retain her. The writer knows an employer in one of the suburbs who built a bay at the back of her house so that her cook might have a pleasant room in which to sleep, and another in which to receive her friends. This employer naturally felt aggrieved when the cook refused to stay in her bay. Viewed in an historic light, this employer might quite as well have added a bay to her house for her shoemaker, and then deemed him ungrateful because he declined to live in it.

A listener, attentive to a conversation between two employers of household labor, — and we certainly all have opportunity to hear such conversations, — would often discover a tone implying that the employer was abused and put upon; that she was struggling with the problem solely because she was thus serving her family and performing her social duties; that otherwise it would be a great relief to her to abandon the entire situation, and "never have a servant in her house again." Did she follow this impulse, she would simply yield to the trend of her times and accept the present system of production. She would be in line with the industrial organization of her age. Were she in line ethically, she would have to believe that the sacredness and beauty of family life do not consist in the processes of the separate preparation of food, but in sharing the corporate life of the community, and in making the family the unit of that life.

The selfishness of a modern mistress, who, in her narrow social ethics, insists that those who minister to the comforts of her family shall minister to it alone, that they shall not only be celibate, but shall be cut off, more or less, from their natural social ties, excludes the best working-people from her service.

A man of dignity and ability is quite willing to come into a house to tune a piano. Another man of mechanical skill will come to put up window shades. Another of less skill, but of perfect independence, will come to clean and relay a carpet. These men would all resent the situation and consider it quite impossible if it implied the giving up of their family and social ties, and living under the roof of the household requiring their services.

The isolation of the household employee is perhaps inevitable so long as the employer holds her belated ethics; but the situation is made even more difficult by the character and capacity of the girls who enter this industry. In any great industrial change the workmen who are permanently displaced are those who are too dull to seize upon changed conditions. The workmen who have knowledge and insight, who are in touch with their time, quickly reorganize.

The general statement may be made that the enterprising girls of the community go into factories, and the less enterprising go into households, although there are many exceptions. It is not a question of skill, of energy, of conscientious work, which will make a girl rise industrially while she is in the household; she is not in the rising move-ment. She is belated in a class composed of the unprogressive elements of the com-munity, which is recruited constantly by those from the ranks of the incompetent, by girls who are learning the language, girls who are timid and slow, or girls who look at life solely from the savings-bank point of view. The distracted housekeeper strug-gles with these unprogressive girls, holding to them not even the well-defined and inde-pendent relation of employer and employed, but the hazy and constantly changing one of mistress to servant.

The latter relation is changing under pressure from various directions. In our increasing democracy the notion of personal service is constantly becoming more dis-tasteful, conflicting, as it does, with the more modern notion of personal dignity. Personal ministration to the needs of childhood, illness, and old age seem to us reasonable, and the democratic adjustment in regard to them is being made. The first two are constantly raised nearer to the level of a profession, and there is little doubt that the third will soon follow. But personal ministrations to a normal, healthy adult, consuming the time and energy of another adult, we find more difficult to reconcile to our theories of democracy.

A factory employer parts with his men at the factory gates at the end of a day's work; they go to their homes as he goes to his, in the assumption that they both do what they want and spend their money as they please; but this solace of equality outside of working hours is denied the bewildered employer of household labor.

She is obliged to live constantly in the same house with her employee, and because of certain equalities in food and shelter she is brought more sharply face to face with the mental and social inequalities.

The difficulty becomes more apparent as the character of the work performed by the so-called servant is less absolutely useful and may be merely time consuming. A kind-hearted woman who will complacently take an afternoon drive, leaving her cook to prepare the five courses of a "little dinner for only ten guests," will not be nearly so comfortable the next evening when she speeds her daughter to a dance, conscious that her waitress must spend the evening in dull solitude on the chance that a caller or two may ring the door-bell.

A conscientious employer once remarked to the writer: " In England it must be much easier; the maid does not look and dress so like your daughter, and you can at least pretend that she doesn't like the same things. But really, my new waitress is quite as pretty and stylish as my daughter is, and her wistful look sometimes when Mary goes off to a frolic quite breaks my heart."

Too many employers of domestic service have always been exempt from manual labor,

and therefore constantly impose exacting duties upon employees, the nature of which they
do not understand by experience; there is
thus no curb of rationality imposed upon the
employer's requirements and demands. She
is totally unlike the foreman in a shop, who
has only risen to his position by way of having actually performed with his own hands
all the work of the men he directs. There
is also another class of employers of domestic labor, who grow capricious and
over-exacting through sheer lack of larger
interests to occupy their minds; it is equally
bad for them and the employee that the
duties of the latter are not clearly defined.
Tolstoy contends that an exaggerated notion
of cleanliness has developed among such
employers, which could never have been
evolved among usefully employed people.
He points to the fact that a serving man, in
order that his hands may be immaculately
clean, is kept from performing the heavier
work of the household, and then is supplied
with a tray, upon which to place a card, in

order that even his clean hands may not touch it; later, even his clean hands are covered with a pair of clean white gloves, which hold the tray upon which the card is placed.

If it were not for the undemocratic ethics used by the employers of domestics, much work now performed in the household would be done outside, as is true of many products formerly manufactured in the feudal household. The worker in all other trades has complete control of his own time after the performance of definitely limited services, his wages are paid altogether in money which he may spend in the maintenance of a separate home life, and he has full opportunity to organize with the other workers in his trade.

The domestic employee is retained in the household largely because her "mistress" fatuously believes that she is thus maintaining the sanctity of family life.

The household employee has no regular opportunity for meeting other workers of her trade, and of attaining with them the dignity of a corporate body. The industrial isolation of the household employee results, as isolation in a trade must always result, in a lack of progress in the methods and products of that trade, and a lack of aspiration and education in the workman. Whether we recognize this isolation as a cause or not, we are all ready to acknowledge that household labor has been in some way belated; that the improvements there have not kept up with the improvement in other occupations. It is said that the last revolution in the processes of cooking was brought about by Count Rumford, who died a hundred years ago. This is largely due to the lack of *esprit de corps* among the employees, which keeps them collectively from fresh achievements, as the absence of education in the individual keeps her from improving her implements.

Under this isolation, not only must one set of utensils serve divers purposes, and, as a consequence, tend to a lessened volume and lower quality of work, but, inasmuch as the appliances are not made to perform the fullest work, there is an amount of capital invested disproportionate to the product when measured by the achievement in other branches of industry. More important than this is the result of the isolation upon the worker herself. There is nothing more devastating to the inventive faculty, nor fatal to a flow of mind and spirit, than the constant feeling of loneliness and the absence of that fellowship which makes our public opinion. If an angry foreman reprimands a girl for breaking a machine, twenty other girls hear him, and the culprit knows perfectly well their opinion as to the justice or injustice of her situation. In either case she bears it better for knowing that, and not thinking it over in solitude. If a household employee breaks a utensil or a piece of porcelain and is reprimanded by her employer, too often the invisible jury is the family of the latter, who naturally uphold her censorious position and intensify the feeling of loneliness in the employee.

The household employee, in addition to her industrial isolation, is also isolated socially. It is well to remember that the household employees for the better quarters of the city and suburbs are largely drawn from the poorer quarters, which are nothing if not gregarious. The girl is born and reared in a tenement house full of children. She goes to school with them, and there she learns to march, to read, and write in companionship with forty others. When she is old enough to go to parties, those she attends are usually held in a public hall and are crowded with dancers. If she works in a factory, she walks home with many other girls, in much the same spirit as she formerly walked to school with them. She mingles with the young men she knows, in frank, economic, and social equality. Until she marries she remains at home with no special break or change in her family and social life. If she is employed in a household, this is not true. Suddenly all the conditions of her life are altered. This change may be wholesome for her, but it is not easy, and thought of the savings-bank does not cheer one much, when one is twenty. She is isolated from the people with whom she has been reared, with whom she has gone to school, and among whom she expects to live when she marries. She is naturally lonely and constrained away from them, and the " new maid " often seems " queer " to her employer's family. She does not care to mingle socially with the people in whose house she is employed, as the girl from the country often does, but she suffers horribly from loneliness.

This wholesome, instinctive dread of social isolation is so strong that, as every city intelligence-office can testify, the filling of situations is easier, or more difficult, in proportion as the place offers more or less companionship. Thus, the easy situation to fill is always the city house, with five or six employees, shading off into the more difficult suburban home, with two, and the utterly impossible lonely country house.

There are suburban employers of household labor who make heroic efforts to supply domestic and social life to their employees; who take the domestic employee to drive, arrange to have her invited out occasionally; who supply her with books and papers and companionship. Nothing could be more praiseworthy in motive, but it is seldom successful in actual operation, resulting as it does in a simulacrum of companionship. The employee may have a genuine friendship for her employer, and a pleasure in her companionship, or she may not have, and the unnaturalness of the situation comes from the insistence that she has, merely because of the propinquity.

The unnaturalness of the situation is intensified by the fact that the employee is practically debarred by distance and lack of leisure from her natural associates, and that her employer sympathetically insists upon filling the vacancy in interests

and affections by her own tastes and friendship. She may or may not succeed, but the
employee should not be thus dependent
upon the good will of her employer. That
in itself is undemocratic.

The difficulty is increasing by a sense of
social discrimination which the household
employee keenly feels is against her and in
favor of the factory girls, in the minds of the
young men of her acquaintance. Women
seeking employment, understand perfectly
well this feeling among mechanics, doubtless
quite unjustifiable, but it acts as a strong in-
ducement toward factory labor. The writer
has long ceased to apologize for the views and
opinions of working people, being quite sure
that on the whole they are quite as wise and
quite as foolish as the views and opinions
of other people, but that this particularly
foolish opinion of young mechanics is widely
shared by the employing class can be easily
demonstrated. The contrast is further ac-
centuated by the better social position of the
factory girl, and the advantages provided for

her in the way of lunch clubs, social clubs, and vacation homes, from which girls performing household labor are practically excluded by their hours of work, their geographical situation, and a curious feeling that they are not as interesting as factory girls.

This separation from her natural social ties affects, of course, her opportunity for family life. It is well to remember that women, as a rule, are devoted to their families; that they want to live with their parents, their brothers and sisters, and kinsfolk, and will sacrifice much to accomplish this. This devotion is so universal that it is impossible to ignore it when we consider women as employees. Young unmarried women are not detached from family claims and requirements as young men are, and are more ready and steady in their response to the needs of aged parents and the helpless members of the family. But women performing labor in households have peculiar difficulties in responding to their family claims, and are practically dependent upon their employers for opportunities of even seeing their relatives and friends.

Curiously enough the same devotion to family life and quick response to its claims, on the part of the employer, operates against the girl employed in household labor, and still further contributes to her isolation.

The employer of household labor, in her zeal to preserve her own family life intact and free from intrusion, acts inconsistently and grants to her cook, for instance, but once or twice a week, such opportunity for untrammelled association with her relatives as the employer's family claims constantly. This in itself is undemocratic, in that it makes a distinction between the value of family life for one set of people as over against another; or, rather, claims that one set of people are of so much less importance than another, that a valuable side of life pertaining to them should be sacrificed for the other.

This cannot be defended theoretically, and no doubt much of the talk among the em-

ployers of household labor, that their employees are carefully shielded and cared for,
and that it is so much better for a girl's health
and morals to work in a household than to
work in a factory, comes from a certain uneasi-
ness of conscience, and from a desire to make
up by individual scruple what would be done
much more freely and naturally by public
opinion if it had an untrammelled chance to
assert itself. One person, or a number of
isolated persons, however conscientious, cannot perform this office of public opinion.
Certain hospitals in London have contributed statistics showing that seventy-eight
per cent of illegitimate children born there
are the children of girls working in households. These girls are certainly not less
virtuous than factory girls, for they come
from the same families and have had the
same training, but the girls who remain at
home and work in factories meet their lovers
naturally and easily, their fathers and brothers know the men, and unconsciously exercise a certain supervision and a certain

direction in their choice of companionship.
The household employees living in another
part of the city, away from their natural
family and social ties, depend upon chance
for the lovers whom they meet. The lover
may be the young man who delivers for the
butcher or grocer, or the solitary friend,
who follows the girl from her own part of
town and pursues unfairly the advantage
which her social loneliness and isolation
afford him. There is no available public
opinion nor any standard of convention which
the girl can apply to her own situation.

It would be easy to point out many incon-
veniences arising from the fact that the old
economic forms are retained when moral
conditions which befitted them have entirely disappeared, but until employers of
domestic labor become conscious of their
narrow code of ethics, and make a distinct
effort to break through the status of mistress and servant, because it shocks their
moral sense, there is no chance of even
beginning a reform.

A fuller social and domestic life among household employees would be steps toward securing their entrance into the larger industrial organizations by which the needs of a community are most successfully administered. Many a girl who complains of loneliness, and who relinquishes her situation with that as her sole excuse, feebly tries to formulate her sense of restraint and social mal-adjustment. She sometimes says that she "feels so unnatural all the time." The writer has known the voice of a girl to change so much during three weeks of "service" that she could not recognize it when the girl returned to her home. It alternated between the high falsetto in which a shy child "speaks a piece" and the husky gulp with which the *globus hystericus* is swallowed. The alertness and *bonhomie* of the voice of the tenement-house child had totally disappeared. When such a girl leaves her employer, her reasons are often incoherent and totally incomprehensible to that good lady, who naturally

concludes that she wishes to get away from
the work and back to her dances and giddy
life, content, if she has these, to stand many
hours in an insanitary factory. The charge
of the employer is only half a truth. These
dances may be the only organized form of
social life which the disheartened employee
is able to mention, but the girl herself, in
her discontent and her moving from place
to place, is blindly striving to respond to a
larger social life. Her employer thinks that
she should be able to consider only the interests and conveniences of her employer's
family, because the employer herself is holding to a family outlook, and refuses to allow
her mind to take in the larger aspects of the
situation.

Although this household industry survives in the midst of the factory system, it
must, of course, constantly compete with
it. Women with little children, or those
with invalids depending upon them, cannot
enter either occupation, and they are practically confined to the sewing trades; but

to all other untrained women seeking employment a choice is open between these two forms of labor.

There are few women so dull that they cannot paste labels on a box, or do some form of factory work; few so dull that some perplexed housekeeper will not receive them, at least for a trial, in her household. Household labor, then, has to compete with factory labor, and women seeking employment, more or less consciously compare these two forms of labor in point of hours, in point of permanency of employment, in point of wages, and in point of the advantage they afford for family and social life. Three points are easily disposed of. First, in regard to hours, there is no doubt that the factory has the advantage. The average factory hours are from seven in the morning to six in the evening, with the chance of working overtime in busy seasons. This leaves most of the evenings and Sundays entirely free. The average hours of household labor are from six in the morning until eight at night, with little difference in seasons. There is one afternoon a week, with an occasional evening, but Sunday is seldom wholly free. Even these evenings and afternoons take the form of a concession from the employer. They are called "evenings out," as if the time really belonged to her, but that she was graciously permitting her employee to use it. This attitude, of course, is in marked contrast to that maintained by the factory operative, who, when she works evenings is paid for "over-time."

Second, in regard to permanency of position, the advantage is found clearly on the side of the household employee, if she proves in any measure satisfactory to her employer, for she encounters much less competition.

Third, in point of wages, the household is again fairly ahead, if we consider not the money received, but the opportunity offered for saving money. This is greater among household employees, because they do not pay board, the clothing required is simpler, and the temptation to spend money in recreation is less frequent. The minimum wages paid an adult in household labor may be fairly put at two dollars and a half a week; the maximum at six dollars, this excluding the comparatively rare opportunities for women to cook at forty dollars a month, and the housekeeper's position at fifty dollars a month.

The factory wages, viewed from the savings-bank point of view, may be smaller in the average, but this is doubtless counterbalanced in the minds of the employees by the greater chance which the factory offers for increased wages. A girl over sixteen seldom works in a factory for less than four dollars a week, and always cherishes the hope of at last being a forewoman with a permanent salary of from fifteen to twenty-five dollars a week. Whether she attains this or not, she runs a fair chance of earning ten dollars a week as a skilled worker. A girl finds it easier to be content with three dollars a week, when she pays for board, in a scale of wages rising toward ten dollars, than to be

content with four dollars a week and pay no
board, in a scale of wages rising toward six
dollars; and the girl well knows that there
are scores of forewomen at sixty dollars a
month for one forty-dollar cook or fifty-dollar
housekeeper. In many cases this position is
well taken economically, for, although the
opportunity for saving may be better for the
employees in the household than in the factory, her family saves more when she works
in a factory and lives with them. The rent is
no more when she is at home. The two
dollars and a half a week which she pays into
the family fund more than covers the cost of
her actual food, and at night she can often
contribute toward the family labor by helping her mother wash and sew.

The fourth point has already been considered, and if the premise in regard to the isolation of the household employee is well taken,
and if the position can be sustained that this
isolation proves the determining factor in the
situation, then certainly an effort should be
made to remedy this, at least in its domestic

and social aspects. To allow household employees to live with their own families and among their own friends, as factory employees now do, would be to relegate more production to industrial centres administered on the factory system, and to secure shorter hours for that which remains to be done in the household.

In those cases in which the household employees have no family ties, doubtless a remedy against social isolation would be the formation of residence clubs, at least in the suburbs, where the isolation is most keenly felt. Indeed, the beginnings of these clubs are already seen in the servants' quarters at the summer hotels. In these residence clubs, the household employee could have the independent life which only one's own abiding place can afford. This, of course, presupposes a higher grade of ability than household employees at present possess; on the other hand, it is only by offering such possibilities that the higher grades of intelligence can be secured for household employment. As the plan of separate clubs for household employees will probably come first in the suburbs, where the difficulty of securing and holding "servants" under the present system is most keenly felt, so the plan of buying cooked food from an outside kitchen, and of having more and more of the household product relegated to the factory, will probably come from the comparatively poor people in the city, who feel most keenly the pressure of the present system. They already consume a much larger proportion of canned goods and bakers' wares and "prepared meats" than the more prosperous people do, because they cannot command the skill nor the time for the more tedious preparation of the raw material. The writer has seen a tenement-house mother pass by a basket of green peas at the door of a local grocery store, to purchase a tin of canned peas, because they could be easily prepared for supper and "the children liked the tinny taste."

It is comparatively easy for an employer to manage her household industry with a cook, a laundress, a waitress. The difficulties really begin when the family income is so small that but one person can be employed in the household for all these varied functions, and the difficulties increase and grow almost insurmountable as they fall altogether upon the mother of the family, who is living in a flat, or, worse still, in a tenement house, where one stove and one set of utensils must be put to all sorts of uses, fit or unfit, making the living room of the family a horror in summer, and perfectly insupportable on rainy washing-days in winter. Such a woman, rather than the prosperous housekeeper, uses factory products, and thus no high standard of quality is established.

The problem of domestic service, which has long been discussed in the United States and England, is now coming to prominence in France. As a well-known economist has recently pointed out, the large defection in the ranks of domestics is there regarded as a sign of revolt against an "unconscious slavery," while English and

American writers appeal to the statistics
which point to the absorption of an enormous number of the class from which servants were formerly recruited into factory
employments, and urge, as the natural solution, that more of the products used in
households be manufactured in factories,
and that personal service, at least for
healthy adults, be eliminated altogether.
Both of these lines of discussion certainly
indicate that domestic service is yielding
to the influence of a democratic movement, and is emerging from the narrower
code of family ethics into the larger code
governing social relations.   It still remains
to express the ethical advance through
changed economic conditions by which the
actual needs of the family may be supplied
not only more effectively but more in line
with associated effort.   To fail to apprehend
the tendency of one's age, and to fail to adapt
the conditions of an industry to it, is to leave
that industry ill-adjusted and belated on the
economic side, and out of line ethically.

CHAPTER V

Industrial Amelioration

THERE is no doubt that the great difficulty we experience in reducing to action our imperfect code of social ethics arises from the fact that we have not yet learned to act together, and find it far from easy even to fuse our principles and aims into a satisfactory statement. We have all been at times entertained by the futile efforts of half a dozen highly individualized people gathered together as a committee. Their aimless attempts to find a common method of action have recalled the wavering motion of a baby's arm before he has learned to coördinate his muscles.

If, as is many times stated, we are passing from an age of individualism to one of association, there is no doubt that for de-

cisive and effective action the individual
still has the best of it. He will secure effi-
cient results while committees are still de-
liberating upon the best method of making
a beginning. And yet, if the need of the
times demand associated effort, it may easily
be true that the action which appears inef-
fective, and yet is carried out upon the more
highly developed line of associated effort,
may represent a finer social quality and
have a greater social value than the more
effective individual action. It is possible
that an individual may be successful, largely
because he conserves all his powers for individual achievement and does not put any
of his energy into the training which will
give him the ability to act with others.
The individual acts promptly, and we are
dazzled by his success while only dimly
conscious of the inadequacy of his code.
Nowhere is this illustrated more clearly
than in industrial relations, as existing between the owner of a large factory and his
employees.

A growing conflict may be detected between the democratic ideal, which urges the workmen to demand representation in the administration of industry, and the accepted position, that the man who owns the capital and takes the risks has the exclusive right of management. It is in reality a clash between individual or aristocratic management, and corporate or democratic management. A large and highly developed factory presents a sharp contrast between its socialized form and individualistic ends.

It is possible to illustrate this difference by a series of events which occurred in Chicago during the summer of 1894. These events epitomized and exaggerated, but at the same time challenged, the code of ethics which regulates much of our daily conduct, and clearly showed that so-called social relations are often resting upon the will of an individual, and are in reality regulated by a code of individual ethics.

As this situation illustrates a point of great difficulty to which we have arrived in our development of social ethics, it may be justifiable to discuss it at some length. Let us recall the facts, not as they have been investigated and printed, but as they remain in our memories.

A large manufacturing company had provided commodious workshops, and, at the instigation of its president, had built a model town for the use of its employees. After a series of years it was deemed necessary, during a financial depression, to reduce the wages of these employees by giving each workman less than full-time work "in order to keep the shops open." This reduction was not accepted by the men, who had become discontented with the factory management and the town regulations, and a strike ensued, followed by a complete shut-down of the works. Although these shops were non-union shops, the strikers were hastily organized and appealed for help to the American

Railway Union, which at that moment was holding its biennial meeting in Chicago. After some days' discussion and some futile attempts at arbitration, a sympathetic strike was declared, which gradually involved railway men in all parts of the country, and orderly transportation was brought to a complete standstill. In the excitement which followed, cars were burned and tracks torn up. The police of Chicago did not cope with the disorder, and the railway companies, apparently distrusting the Governor of the State, and in order to protect the United States mails, called upon the President of the United States for the federal troops, the federal courts further enjoined all persons against any form of interference with the property or operation of the railroads, and the situation gradually assumed the proportions of internecine warfare. During all of these events the president of the manufacturing company first involved, steadfastly refused to have the situation submitted to arbitration, and this attitude naturally provoked much discussion. The discussion was broadly divided between those who held that the long kindness of the president of the company had been most ungratefully received, and those who maintained that the situation was the inevitable outcome of the social consciousness developing among working people. The first defended the president of the company in his persistent refusal to arbitrate, maintaining that arbitration was impossible after the matter had been taken up by other than his own employees, and they declared that a man must be allowed to run his own business. They considered the firm stand of the president a service to the manufacturing interests of the entire country. The others claimed that a large manufacturing concern has ceased to be a private matter; that not only a number of workmen and stockholders are concerned in its management, but that the interests of the public are so involved that the officers of the company are in a real sense administering a public trust.

This prolonged strike clearly puts in a concrete form the ethics of an individual, in this case a benevolent employer, and the ethics of a mass of men, his employees, claiming what they believed to be their moral rights.

These events illustrate the difficulty of managing an industry which has become organized into a vast social operation, not with the coöperation of the workman thus socialized, but solely by the dictation of the individual owning the capital. There is a sharp divergence between the social form and the individual aim, which becomes greater as the employees are more highly socialized and dependent. The president of the company under discussion went further than the usual employer does. He socialized not only the factory, but the form in which his workmen were living. He built, and in a great measure regulated, an entire town, without calling upon the workmen either for self-expression or self-government. He honestly believed that he knew better than they what was for their good, as he certainly knew better than they how to conduct his business. As his factory developed and increased, making money each year under his direction, he naturally expected the town to prosper in the same way.

He did not realize that the men submitted to the undemocratic conditions of the factory organization because the economic pressure in our industrial affairs is so great that they could not do otherwise. Under this pressure they could be successfully discouraged from organization, and systematically treated on the individual basis.

Social life, however, in spite of class distinctions, is much freer than industrial life, and the men resented the extension of industrial control to domestic and social arrangements. They felt the lack of democracy in the assumption that they should be taken care of in these matters, in which even the humblest workman has won his independence. The basic difficulty lay in the fact that an individual was directing the social affairs of many men without any consistent effort to find out their desires, and without any organization through which to give them social expression. The president of the company was, moreover, so confident of the righteousness of his aim that he had come to test the righteousness of the process by his own feelings and not by those of the men. He doubtless built the town from a sincere desire to give his employees the best surroundings. As it developed, he gradually took toward it the artist attitude toward his own creation, which has no thought for the creation itself but is absorbed in the idea it stands for, and he ceased to measure the usefulness of the town by the standard of the men's needs. This process slowly darkened his glints of memory, which might have connected his experience with that of his men. It is possible to cultivate the impulses of the benefactor until the power of attaining a simple human relationship with the beneficiaries, that of frank equality with them, is gone, and there is left no mutual interest in a common cause. To perform too many good deeds may be to lose the power of recognizing good in others; to be too absorbed in carrying out a personal plan of improvement may be to fail to catch the great moral lesson which our times offer.

The president of this company fostered his employees for many years; he gave them sanitary houses and beautiful parks; but in their extreme need, when they were struggling with the most difficult situation which the times could present to them, he lost his touch and had nothing wherewith to help them. The employer's conception of goodness for his men had been cleanliness, decency of living, and, above all, thrift and temperance. Means had been provided for all this, and opportunities had also been given for recreation and improvement. But this employer suddenly found his town in the sweep of a world-wide moral impulse. A movement had been going on about him and among his working men, of which he had been unconscious, or concerning which he had heard only by rumor.

Outside the ken of philanthropists the proletariat had learned to say in many languages, that "the injury of one is the concern of all." Their watchwords were brotherhood, sacrifice, the subordination of individual and trade interests, to the good of the working classes, and they were moved by a determination to free that class from the untoward conditions under which they were laboring.

Compared to these watchwords, the old ones which this philanthropic employer had given his town were negative and inadequate. He had believed strongly in temperance and steadiness of individual effort, but had failed to apprehend the greater movement of combined abstinence and concerted action. With all his fostering, the president had not attained to a conception of social morality for his men and had imagined that virtue for them largely meant absence of vice.

When the labor movement finally stirred his town, or, to speak more fairly, when, in their distress and perplexity, his own employees appealed to an organized manifestation of this movement, they were quite sure that simply because they were workmen in distress they would not be deserted by it. This loyalty on the part of a widely ramified and well-organized union toward the workmen in a "non-union shop," who had contributed nothing to its cause, was certainly a manifestation of moral power.

In none of his utterances or correspondence did the president for an instant recognize this touch of nobility, although one would imagine that he would gladly point out this bit of virtue, in what he must have considered the moral ruin about him. He stood throughout for the individual virtues, those which had distinguished the model workmen of his youth; those which had enabled him and so many of his contemporaries to rise in life, when "rising in life" was urged upon every promising boy as the goal of his efforts.

Of the code of social ethics he had caught absolutely nothing. The morals he had advocated in selecting and training his men did not fail them in the hour of confusion. They were self-controlled, and they themselves destroyed no property. They were sober and exhibited no drunkenness, even although obliged to hold their meetings in the saloon hall of a neighboring town. They repaid their employer in kind, but he had given them no rule for the life of association into which they were plunged.

The president of the company desired that his employees should possess the individual and family virtues, but did nothing to cherish in them the social virtues which express themselves in associated effort.

Day after day, during that horrible time of suspense, when the wires constantly reported the same message, "the President of the Company holds that there is nothing to arbitrate," one was forced to feel that the ideal of one-man rule was being sustained in its baldest form. A demand from many parts of the country and from many people was being made for social adjustment, against which the commercial training and the individualistic point of view held its own successfully.

The majority of the stockholders, not only of this company but of similar companies, and many other citizens, who had had the same commercial experience, shared and sustained this position. It was quite impossible for them to catch the other point of view. They not only felt themselves right from the commercial standpoint, but had gradually accustomed themselves also to the philanthropic standpoint, until they had come to consider their motives beyond reproach. Habit held them persistent in this view of the case through all changing conditions.

A wise man has said that "the consent

of men and your own conscience are two wings given you whereby you may rise to God." It is so easy for the good and powerful to think that they can rise by following the dictates of conscience, by pursuing their own ideals, that they are prone to leave those ideals unconnected with the consent of their fellow-men. The president of the company thought out within his own mind a beautiful town. He had power with which to build this town, but he did not appeal to nor obtain the consent of the men who were living in it. The most unambitious reform, recognizing the necessity for this consent, makes for slow but sane and strenuous progress, while the most ambitious of social plans and experiments, ignoring this, is prone to failure.

The man who insists upon consent, who moves with the people, is bound to consult the "feasible right" as well as the absolute right. He is often obliged to attain only Mr. Lincoln's " best possible," and then has the sickening sense of compromise with his best convictions. He has to move along

with those whom he leads toward a goal
that neither he nor they see very clearly till
they come to it. He has to discover what
people really want, and then "provide the
channels in which the growing moral force
of their lives shall flow." What he does
attain, however, is not the result of his
individual striving, as a solitary mountain-
climber beyond that of the valley multitude
but it is sustained and upheld by the
sentiments and aspirations of many others.
Progress has been slower perpendicularly,
but incomparably greater because lateral.
He has not taught his contemporaries to
climb mountains, but he has persuaded the
villagers to move up a few feet higher;
added to this, he has made secure his progress. A few months after the death of the
promoter of this model town, a court decision made it obligatory upon the company
to divest itself of the management of the
town as involving a function beyond its
corporate powers. The parks, flowers, and
fountains of this far-famed industrial centre

INDUSTRIAL AMELIORATION

were dismantled, with scarcely a protest from the inhabitants themselves.

The man who disassociates his ambition, however disinterested, from the coöperation of his fellows, always takes this risk of ultimate failure. He does not take advantage of the great conserver and guarantee of his own permanent success which associated efforts afford. Genuine experiments toward higher social conditions must have a more democratic faith and practice than those which underlie private venture. Public parks and improvements, intended for the common use, are after all only safe in the hands of the public itself; and associated effort toward social progress, although much more awkward and stumbling than that same effort managed by a capable individual, does yet enlist deeper forces and evoke higher social capacities.

The successful business man who is also the philanthropist is in more than the usual danger of getting widely separated from his employees. The men already have the

American veneration for wealth and successful business capacity, and, added to this, they are dazzled by his good works. The workmen have the same kindly impulses as he, but while they organize their charity into mutual benefit associations and distribute their money in small amounts in relief for the widows and insurance for the injured, the employer may build model towns, erect college buildings, which are tangible and enduring, and thereby display his goodness in concentrated form.

By the very exigencies of business demands, the employer is too often cut off from the social ethics developing in regard to our larger social relationships, and from the great moral life springing from our common experiences. This is sure to happen when he is good "to" people rather than "with" them, when he allows himself to decide what is best for them instead of consulting them. He thus misses the rectifying influence of that fellowship which is so big that it leaves no room for sensitiveness or gratitude. Without this fellowship we may never know how great the divergence between ourselves and others may become, nor how cruel the misunderstandings.

During a recent strike of the employees of a large factory in Ohio, the president of the company expressed himself as bitterly disappointed by the results of his many kindnesses, and evidently considered the employees utterly unappreciative. His state of mind was the result of the fallacy of ministering to social needs from an individual impulse and expecting a socialized return of gratitude and loyalty. If the lunch-room was necessary, it was a necessity in order that the employees might have better food, and, when they had received the better food, the legitimate aim of the lunch-room was met. If baths were desirable, and the fifteen minutes of calisthenic exercise given the women in the middle of each half day brought a needed rest and change to their muscles, then the increased cleanliness and the increased bodily

155

comfort of so many people should of themselves have justified the experiment.

To demand, as a further result, that there
should be no strikes in the factory, no revolt
against the will of the employer because the
employees were filled with loyalty as the
result of the kindness, was of course to take
the experiment from an individual basis to
a social one.

Large mining companies and manufacturing concerns are constantly appealing to
their stockholders for funds, or for permission to take a percentage of the profits, in
order that the money may be used for educational and social schemes designed for the
benefit of the employees. The promoters
of these schemes use as an argument and as
an appeal, that better relations will be thus
established, that strikes will be prevented, and
that in the end the money returned to the
stockholders will be increased. However
praiseworthy this appeal may be in motive, it
involves a distinct confusion of issues, and
in theory deserves the failure it so often

meets with in practice. In the clash which follows a strike, the employees are accused of an ingratitude, when there was no legitimate reason to expect gratitude; and useless bitterness, which has really a factitious basis, may be developed on both sides.

Indeed, unless the relation becomes a democratic one, the chances of misunderstanding are increased, when to the relation of employer and employees is added the relation of benefactor to beneficiaries, in so far as there is still another opportunity for acting upon the individual code of ethics.

There is no doubt that these efforts are to be commended, not only from the standpoint of their social value but because they have a marked industrial significance. Failing, as they do, however, to touch the question of wages and hours, which are almost invariably the points of trades-union effort, the employers confuse the mind of the public when they urge the amelioration of conditions and the kindly relation existing between them and their men as a reason for the discontinuance of strikes and other trades-union tactics. The men have individually accepted the kindness of the employers as it was individually offered, but quite as the latter urges his inability to increase wages unless he has the coöperation of his competitors, so the men state that they are bound to the trades-union struggle for an increase in wages because it can only be undertaken by combinations of labor.

Even the much more democratic effort to divide a proportion of the profits at the end of the year among the employees, upon the basis of their wages and efficiency, is also exposed to a weakness, from the fact that the employing side has the power of determining to whom the benefit shall accrue.

Both individual acts of self-defence on the part of the wage earner and individual acts of benevolence on the part of the employer are most useful as they establish standards to which the average worker and employer may in time be legally compelled to conform. Progress must always come through the individual who varies from the type and has sufficient energy to express this variation. He first holds a higher conception than that held by the mass of his fellows of what is righteous under given conditions, and expresses this conviction in conduct, in many instances formulating a certain scruple which the others share, but have not yet defined even to themselves. Progress, however, is not secure until the mass has conformed to this new righteousness. This is equally true in regard to any advance made in the standard of living on the part of the trades-unionists or in the improved conditions of industry on the part of reforming employers. The mistake lies, not in overpraising the advance thus inaugurated by individual initiative, but in regarding the achievement as complete in a social sense when it is still in the realm of individual action.

No sane manufacturer regards his factory as the centre of the industrial system. He knows very well that the cost of material, wages, and selling prices are determined by industrial conditions completely beyond his control. Yet the same man may quite calmly regard himself and his own private principles as merely self-regarding, and expect results from casual philanthropy which can only be accomplished through those common rules of life and labor established by the community for the common good.

Outside of and surrounding these smaller and most significant efforts are the larger and irresistible movements operating toward combination. This movement must tend to decide upon social matters from the social standpoint. Until then it is difficult to keep our minds free from a confusion of issues. Such a confusion occurs when the gift of a large sum to the community for a public and philanthropic purpose, throws a certain glamour over all the earlier acts of a man, and makes it difficult for the community to see possible wrongs committed against it, in the accumulation of wealth so beneficently used. It is possible also that the resolve to be thus generous unconsciously influences the man himself in his methods of accumulation. He keeps to a certain individual rectitude, meaning to make an individual restitution by the old paths of generosity and kindness, whereas if he had in view social restitution on the newer lines of justice and opportunity, he would throughout his course doubtless be watchful of his industrial relationships and his social virtues.

The danger of professionally attaining to the power of the righteous man, of yielding to the ambition "for doing good" on a large scale, compared to which the ambition for politics, learning, or wealth, are vulgar and commonplace, ramifies through our modern life; and those most easily beset by this temptation are precisely the men best situated to experiment on the larger social lines, because they so easily dramatize their acts and lead public opinion. Very often, too, they have in their hands the preservation and advancement of large vested interests, and often see clearly and truly that they are better able to administer the affairs of the community than the community itself: sometimes they see that if they do not administer them sharply and quickly, as only an individual can, certain interests of theirs dependent upon the community will go to ruin.

The model employer first considered, provided a large sum in his will with which to build and equip a polytechnic school, which will doubtless be of great public value. This again shows the advantage of individual management, in the spending as well as in the accumulating of wealth, but this school will attain its highest good, in so far as it incites the ambition to provide other schools from public funds. The town of Zurich possesses a magnificent polytechnic institute, secured by the vote of the entire people and supported from public taxes. Every man who voted for it is interested that his child should enjoy its benefits, and, of course, the voluntary attendance must be larger than in a school accepted as a gift to the community.

In the educational efforts of model employers, as in other attempts toward social amelioration, one man with the best of intentions is trying to do what the entire body of employees should have undertaken to do for themselves. The result of his efforts will only attain its highest value as it serves as an incentive to procure other results by the community as well as for the community.

There are doubtless many things which the public would never demand unless they were first supplied by individual initiative, both because the public lacks the imagination, and also the power of formulating their wants. Thus philanthropic effort supplies kindergartens, until they become so established in the popular affections that they are incorporated in the public school system. Churches and missions establish reading rooms, until at last the public library system dots the city with branch reading rooms and libraries. For this willingness to take risks for the sake of an ideal, for those experiments which must be undertaken with vigor and boldness in order to secure didactic value in failure as well as in success, society must depend upon the individual possessed with money, and also distinguished by earnest and unselfish purpose. Such experiments enable the nation to use the Referendum method in its public affairs. Each social experiment is thus tested by a few people, given wide publicity, that it may be observed and discussed by the bulk of the citizens before the public prudently makes up its mind whether or not it is wise to incorporate it into the functions of government. If the decision is in its favor and it is so incorporated, it can then be carried on with confidence and enthusiasm.

But experience has shown that we can only depend upon successful men for a certain type of experiment in the line of industrial amelioration and social advancement.

The list of those who found churches, educational institutions, libraries, and art galleries, is very long, as is again the list of those contributing to model dwellings, recreation halls, and athletic fields. At the present moment factory employers are doing much to promote "industrial betterment" in the way of sanitary surroundings, opportunities for bathing, lunch rooms provided with cheap and wholesome food, club rooms, and guild halls. But there is a line of social experiment involving social righteousness in its most advanced form, in which the number of employers and the "favored class" are so few that it is plain society cannot count upon them for continuous and valuable help. This lack is in the line of factory legislation and that sort of social advance implied in shorter hours and the regulation of wages; in short, all that organization and activity that is involved in such a maintenance and increase of wages as would prevent the lowering of the standard of life.

A large body of people feel keenly that

the present industrial system is in a state of profound disorder, and that there is no guarantee that the pursuit of individual ethics will ever right it. They claim that relief can only come through deliberate corporate effort inspired by social ideas and guided by the study of economic laws, and that the present industrial system thwarts our ethical demands, not only for social righteousness but for social order. Because they believe that each advance in ethics must be made fast by a corresponding advance in politics and legal enactment, they insist upon the right of state regulation and control. While many people representing all classes in a community would assent to this as to a general proposition, and would even admit it as a certain moral obligation, legislative enactments designed to control industrial conditions have largely been secured through the efforts of a few citizens, mostly those who constantly see the harsh conditions of labor and who are incited to activity by their sympathies as well as their convictions.

This may be illustrated by the series of legal enactments regulating the occupations in which children may be allowed to work, also the laws in regard to the hours of labor permitted in those occupations, and the minimum age below which children may not be employed. The first child labor laws were enacted in England through the efforts of those members of parliament whose hearts were wrung by the condition of the little parish apprentices bound out to the early textile manufacturers of the north; and through the long years required to build up the code of child labor legislation which England now possesses, knowledge of the conditions has always preceded effective legislation. The efforts of that small number in every community who believe in legislative control have always been reënforced by the efforts of trades-unionists rather than by the efforts of employers. Partly because the employment of workingmen in the factories brings them in contact with the children who tend to lower wages and demoralize

their trades, and partly because workingmen have no money nor time to spend in
alleviating philanthropy, and must perforce
seize upon agitation and legal enactment as
the only channel of redress which is open
to them.

We may illustrate by imagining a row
of people seated in a moving street-car,
into which darts a boy of eight, calling out
the details of the last murder, in the hope
of selling an evening newspaper. A comfortable looking man buys a paper from
him with no sense of moral shock; he may
even be a trifle complacent that he has
helped along the little fellow, who is making
his way in the world. The philanthropic
lady sitting next to him may perhaps reflect
that it is a pity that such a bright boy is
not in school. She may make up her mind
in a moment of compunction to redouble
her efforts for various newsboys' schools
and homes, that this poor child may have
better teaching, and perhaps a chance at
manual training. She probably is con-

vinced that he alone, by his unaided efforts, is supporting a widowed mother, and her heart is moved to do all she can for him. Next to her sits a workingman trained in trades-union methods. He knows that the boy's natural development is arrested, and that the abnormal activity of his body and mind uses up the force which should go into growth; moreover, that this premature use of his powers has but a momentary and specious value. He is forced to these conclusions because he has seen many a man, entering the factory at eighteen and twenty, so worn out by premature work that he was "laid on the shelf" within ten or fifteen years. He knows very well that he can do nothing in the way of ameliorating the lot of this particular boy; that his only possible chance is to agitate for proper child-labor laws; to regulate, and if possible prohibit, street-vending by children, in order that the child of the poorest may have his school time secured to him, and may have at least his short chance for growth.

These three people, sitting in the street car, are all honest and upright, and recognize a certain duty toward the forlorn children of the community. The self-made man is encouraging one boy's own efforts; the philanthropic lady is helping on a few boys; the workingman alone is obliged to include all the boys of his class. Workingmen, because of their feebleness in all but numbers, have been forced to appeal to the state, in order to secure protection for themselves and for their children. They cannot all rise out of their class, as the occasionally successful man has done; some of them must be left to do the work in the factories and mines, and they have no money to spend in philanthropy.

Both public agitation and a social appeal to the conscience of the community is necessary in order to secure help from the state, and, curiously enough, child-labor laws once enacted and enforced are a matter of great pride, and even come to be regarded as a register of the community's humanity and enlightenment. If the method of public agitation could find quiet and orderly expression in legislative enactment, and if labor measures could be submitted to the examination and judgment of the whole without a sense of division or of warfare, we should have the ideal development of the democratic state.

But we judge labor organizations as we do other living institutions, not by their declaration of principles, which we seldom read, but by their blundering efforts to apply their principles to actual conditions, and by the oft-time failure of their representatives, when the individual finds himself too weak to become the organ of corporate action.

The very blunders and lack of organization too often characterizing a union, in marked contrast to the orderly management of a factory, often confuse us as to the real issues involved, and we find it hard to trust uncouth and unruly manifestations of social effort. The situation is made even more complicated by the fact that

those who are formulating a code of associated action so often break through the
established code of law and order. As
society has a right to demand of the reforming individual that he be sternly held
to his personal and domestic claims, so it
has a right to insist that labor organizations shall keep to the hardly won standards
of public law and order; and the community
performs but its plain duty when it registers
its protest every time law and order are
subverted, even in the interest of the so-
called social effort. Yet in moments of
industrial stress and strain the community
is confronted by a moral perplexity which
may arise from the mere fact that the good
of yesterday is opposed to the good of to-
day, and that which may appear as a choice
between virtue and vice is really but a choice
between virtue and virtue. In the disorder
and confusion sometimes incident to growth
and progress, the community may be unable
to see anything but the unlovely struggle
itself.

The writer recalls a conversation between two workingmen who were leaving a lecture on "Organic Evolution." The first was much puzzled, and anxiously inquired of the second "if evolution could mean that one animal turned into another." The challenged workman stopped in the rear of the hall, put his foot upon a chair, and expounded what he thought evolution did mean; and this, so nearly as the conversation can be recalled, is what he said: "You see a lot of fishes are living in a stream, which overflows in the spring and strands some of them upon the bank. The weak ones die up there, but others make a big effort to get back into the water. They dig their fins into the sand, breathe as much air as they can with their gills, and have a terrible time. But after a while their fins turn into legs and their gills into lungs, and they have become frogs. Of course they are further along than the sleek, comfortable fishes who sail up and down the stream waving their tails and

despising the poor damaged things thrash-
ing around on the bank. He — the lecturer — did not say anything about men,
but it is easy enough to think of us poor
devils on the dry bank, struggling without
enough to live on, while the comfortable
fellows sail along in the water with all
they want and despise us because we thrash
about." His listener did not reply, and was
evidently dissatisfied both with the explanation and the application. Doubtless the illustration was bungling in more than its setting
forth, but the story is suggestive.

At times of social disturbance the law-
abiding citizen is naturally so anxious for
peace and order, his sympathies are so
justly and inevitably on the side making
for the restoration of law, that it is difficult for him to see the situation fairly.
He becomes insensible to the unselfish
impulse which may prompt a sympathetic
strike in behalf of the workers in a non-
union shop, because he allows his mind to
dwell exclusively on the disorder which has

become associated with the strike. He is completely side-tracked by the ugly phases of a great moral movement. It is always a temptation to assume that the side which has respectability, authority, and superior intelligence, has therefore righteousness as well, especially when the same side presents concrete results of individual effort as over against the less tangible results of associated effort.

It is as yet most difficult for us to free ourselves from the individualistic point of view sufficiently to group events in their social relations and to judge fairly those who are endeavoring to produce a social result through all the difficulties of associated action. The philanthropist still finds his path much easier than do those who are attempting a social morality. In the first place, the public, anxious to praise what it recognizes as an undoubted moral effort often attended with real personal sacrifice, joyfully seizes upon this manifestation and overpraises it, recognizing the philanthropist

as an old friend in the paths of righteousness, whereas the others are strangers and
possibly to be distrusted as aliens. It is
easy to confuse the response to an abnormal
number of individual claims with the response to the social claim. An exaggerated
personal morality is often mistaken for a
social morality, and until it attempts to minister to a social situation its total inadequacy
is not discovered. To attempt to attain a
social morality without a basis of democratic
experience results in the loss of the only
possible corrective and guide, and ends in
an exaggerated individual morality but not
in social morality at all. We see this from
time to time in the care-worn and overworked philanthropist, who has taxed his
individual will beyond the normal limits and
has lost his clew to the situation among a
bewildering number of cases. A man who
takes the betterment of humanity for his
aim and end must also take the daily experiences of humanity for the constant correction of his process. He must not only

test and guide his achievement by human experience, but he must succeed or fail in proportion as he has incorporated that experience with his own. Otherwise his own achievements become his stumbling-block, and he comes to believe in his own goodness as something outside of himself. He makes an exception of himself, and thinks that he is different from the rank and file of his fellows. He forgets that it is necessary to know of the lives of our contemporaries, not only in order to believe in their integrity, which is after all but the first beginnings of social morality, but in order to attain to any mental or moral integrity for ourselves or any such hope for society.

CHAPTER VI

EDUCATIONAL METHODS

As democracy modifies our conception of life, it constantly raises the value and function of each member of the community, however humble he may be. We have come to believe that the most "brutish man" has a value in our common life, a function to perform which can be fulfilled by no one else. We are gradually requiring of the educator that he shall free the powers of each man and connect him with the rest of life. We ask this not merely because it is the man's right to be thus connected, but because we have become convinced that the social order cannot afford to get along without his special contribution. Just as we have come to resent all hindrances which keep us from untrammelled comradeship with our fellows, and as we throw down unnatural divisions, not in the spirit of the eighteenth-century reformers, but in the spirit of those to whom social equality has become a necessity for further social development, so we are impatient to use the dynamic power residing in the mass of men, and demand that the educator free that power. We believe that man's moral idealism is the constructive force of progress, as it has always been; but because every human being is a creative agent and a possible generator of fine enthusiasm, we are sceptical of the moral idealism of the few and demand the education of the many, that there may be greater freedom, strength, and subtilty of intercourse and hence an increase of dynamic power. We are not content to include all men in our hopes, but have become conscious that all men are hoping and are part of the same movement of which we are a part.

Many people impelled by these ideas have become impatient with the slow recognition

on the part of the educators of their mani-
fest obligation to prepare and nourish the
child and the citizen for social relations.
The educators should certainly conserve the
learning and training necessary for the successful individual and family life, but should
add to that a preparation for the enlarged
social efforts which our increasing democracy requires. The democratic ideal demands of the school that it shall give the
child's own experience a social value; that
it shall teach him to direct his own activities and adjust them to those of other
people. We are not willing that thousands
of industrial workers shall put all of their
activity and toil into services from which
the community as a whole reaps the benefit,
while their mental conceptions and code of
morals are narrow and untouched by any
uplift which the consciousness of social
value might give them.

We are impatient with the schools which
lay all stress on reading and writing, sus-
pecting them to rest upon the assumption

that the ordinary experience of life is worth little, and that all knowledge and interest must be brought to the children through the medium of books. Such an assumption fails to give the child any clew to the life about him, or any power to usefully or intelligently connect himself with it. This may be illustrated by observations made in a large Italian colony situated in Chicago, the children from which are, for the most part, sent to the public schools.

The members of the Italian colony are largely from South Italy, — Calabrian and Sicilian peasants, or Neapolitans from the workingmen's quarters of that city. They have come to America with the distinct aim of earning money, and finding more room for the energies of themselves and their children. In almost all cases they mean to go back again, simply because their imaginations cannot picture a continuous life away from the old surroundings. Their experiences in Italy have been those of simple outdoor activity, and their ideas have come directly to them from their struggle with Nature, — such a hand-to-hand struggle as takes place when each man gets his living largely through his own cultivation of the soil, or with tools simply fashioned by his own hands. The women, as in all primitive life, have had more diversified activities than the men. They have cooked, spun, and knitted, in addition to their almost equal work in the fields. Very few of the peasant men or women can either read or write. They are devoted to their children, strong in their family feeling, even to remote relationships, and clannish in their community life.

The entire family has been upheaved, and is striving to adjust itself to its new surroundings. The men, for the most part, work on railroad extensions through the summer, under the direction of a *padrone*, who finds the work for them, regulates the amount of their wages, and supplies them with food. The first effect of immigration upon the women is that of idleness. They no longer work in the fields, nor milk the goats, nor pick up faggots. The mother of the family buys all the clothing, not only already spun and woven but made up into garments, of a cut and fashion beyond her powers. It is, indeed, the most economical thing for her to do. Her house-cleaning and cooking are of the simplest; the bread is usually baked outside of the house, and the macaroni bought prepared for boiling. All of those outdoor and domestic activities, which she would naturally have handed on to her daughters, have slipped away from her. The domestic arts are gone, with their absorbing interests for the children, their educational value, and incentive to activity. A household in a tenement receives almost no raw material. For the hundreds of children who have never seen wheat grow, there are dozens who have never seen bread baked. The occasional washings and scrubbings are associated only with discomfort. The child of such a family receives constant stimulus of most exciting sort from his city

street life, but he has little or no opportunity to use his energies in domestic
manufacture, or, indeed, constructively in
any direction. No activity is supplied to
take the place of that which, in Italy, he
would naturally have found in his own
surroundings, and no new union with wholesome life is made for him.

Italian parents count upon the fact that
their children learn the English language
and American customs before they do themselves, and the children act not only as
interpreters of the language, but as buf-
fers between them and Chicago, resulting
in a certain almost pathetic dependence
of the family upon the child. When a
child of the family, therefore, first goes to
school, the event is fraught with much
significance to all the others. The family
has no social life in any structural form
and can supply none to the child. He
ought to get it in the school and give it
to his family, the school thus becoming
the connector with the organized society

about them. It is the children aged six, eight, and ten, who go to school, entering, of course, the primary grades. If a boy is twelve or thirteen on his arrival in America, his parents see in him a wage-earning factor, and the girl of the same age is already looking toward her marriage.

Let us take one of these boys, who has learned in his six or eight years to speak his native language, and to feel himself strongly identified with the fortunes of his family. Whatever interest has come to the minds of his ancestors has come through the use of their hands in the open air; and open air and activity of body have been the inevitable accompaniments of all their experiences. Yet the first thing that the boy must do when he reaches school is to sit still, at least part of the time, and he must learn to listen to what is said to him, with all the perplexity of listening to a foreign tongue. He does not find this very stimulating, and is slow to respond to the more subtle incentives of the schoolroom. The

peasant child is perfectly indifferent to showing off and making a good recitation. He
leaves all that to his schoolfellows, who are
more sophisticated and equipped with better
English. His parents are not deeply interested in keeping him in school, and will
not hold him there against his inclination.
Their experience does not point to the
good American tradition that it is the
educated man who finally succeeds. The
richest man in the Italian colony can neither
read nor write — even Italian. His cunning
and acquisitiveness, combined with the cre-
dulity and ignorance of his countrymen,
have slowly brought about his large fortune.
The child himself may feel the stirring of
a vague ambition to go on until he is as
the other children are; but he is not popular
with his schoolfellows, and he sadly feels
the lack of dramatic interest. Even the
pictures and objects presented to him, as
well as the language, are strange.

If we admit that in education it is necessary to begin with the experiences which

the child already has and to use his spontaneous and social activity, then the city streets begin this education for him in a more natural way than does the school. The South Italian peasant comes from a life of picking olives and oranges, and he easily sends his children out to pick up coal from railroad tracks, or wood from buildings which have been burned down. Unfortunately, this process leads by easy transition to petty thieving. It is easy to go from the coal on the railroad track to the coal and wood which stand before a dealer's shop; from the potatoes which have rolled from a rumbling wagon to the vegetables displayed by the grocer. This is apt to be the record of the boy who responds constantly to the stimulus and temptations of the street, although in the beginning his search for bits of food and fuel was prompted by the best of motives.

The school has to compete with a great deal from the outside in addition to the distractions of the neighborhood. Nothing is more fascinating than that mysterious "down town," whither the boy longs to go to sell papers and black boots, to attend theatres, and, if possible, to stay all night on the pretence of waiting for the early edition of the great dailies. If a boy is once thoroughly caught in these excitements, nothing can save him from over-stimulation and consequent debility and worthlessness; he arrives at maturity with no habits of regular work and with a distaste for its dulness.

On the other hand, there are hundreds of boys of various nationalities who conscientiously remain in school and fulfil all the requirements of the early grades, and at the age of fourteen are found in factories, painstakingly performing their work year after year. These later are the men who form the mass of the population in every industrial neighborhood of every large city; but they carry on the industrial processes year after year without in the least knowing what it is all about. The one fixed habit which the boy carries away with him from the school to the factory is the feeling that his work is merely provisional. In school the next grade was continually held before him as an object of attainment, and it resulted in the conviction that the sole object of present effort is to get ready for something else. This tentative attitude takes the last bit of social stimulus out of his factory work; he pursues it merely as a necessity, and his very mental attitude destroys his chance for a realization of its social value. As the boy in school contracted the habit of doing his work in certain hours and taking his pleasure in certain other hours, so in the factory he earns his money by ten hours of dull work and spends it in three hours of lurid and unprofitable pleasure in the evening. Both in the school and in the factory, in proportion as his work grows dull and monotonous, his recreation must become more exciting and stimulating. The hopelessness of adding evening classes and social entertainments as a mere frill to a day filled with monotonous and deadening drudgery constantly becomes more apparent to those who are endeavoring to bring a fuller life to the industrial members of the community, and who are looking forward to a time when work shall cease to be senseless drudgery with no self-expression on the part of the worker. It sometimes seems that the public schools should contribute much more than they do to the consummation of this time. If the army of school children who enter the factories every year possessed thoroughly vitalized faculties, they might do much to lighten this incubus of dull factory work which presses so heavily upon so large a number of our fellow-citizens. Has our commercialism been so strong that our schools have become insensibly commercialized, whereas we supposed that our industrial life was receiving the broadening and illuminating effects of the schools? The training of these children, so far as it has been vocational at all, has been in the direction of clerical work. It is possible that the business men, whom we in America so tremendously admire, have really been dictating the curriculum of our public schools, in spite of the conventions of educators and the suggestions of university professors. The business man, of course, has not said, " I will have the public schools train office boys and clerks so that I may have them easily and cheaply," but he has sometimes said, " Teach the children to write legibly and to figure accurately and quickly; to acquire habits of punctuality and order; to be prompt to obey; and you will fit them to make their way in the world as I have made mine." Has the workingman been silent as to what he desires for his children, and allowed the business man to decide for him there, as he has allowed the politician to manage his municipal affairs, or has the workingman so far shared our universal optimism that he has really believed that his children would never need to go into industrial life at all, but that all of his sons would become bankers and merchants?

Certain it is that no sufficient study has been made of the child who enters into industrial life early and stays there permanently, to give him some offset to its monotony and dulness, some historic significance of the part he is taking in the life of the community.

It is at last on behalf of the average workingmen that our increasing democracy impels us to make a new demand upon the educator. As the political expression of democracy has claimed for the workingman the free right of citizenship, so a code of social ethics is now insisting that he shall be a conscious member of society, having some notion of his social and industrial value.

The early ideal of a city that it was a market-place in which to exchange produce, and a mere trading-post for merchants, apparently still survives in our minds and is constantly reflected in our schools. We have either failed to realize that cities have become great centres of production and manufacture in which a huge population is engaged, or we have lacked sufficient presence of mind to adjust ourselves to the change. We admire much more the men who accumulate riches, and who gather to themselves the results of industry, than the men who actually carry forward industrial processes; and, as has been pointed out, our schools still prepare children almost exclusively for commercial and professional life.

Quite as the country boy dreams of leaving the farm for life in town and begins early to imitate the travelling salesman in dress and manner, so the school boy within the town hopes to be an office boy, and later a clerk or salesman, and looks upon work in the factory as the occupation of ignorant and unsuccessful men. The schools do so little really to interest the child in the life of production, or to excite his ambition in the line of industrial occupation, that the ideal of life, almost from the very beginning, becomes not an absorbing interest in one's work and a consciousness of its value and social relation, but a desire for money with which unmeaning purchases may be made and an unmeaning social standing obtained.

The son of a workingman who is successful in commercial life, impresses his family and neighbors quite as does the prominent city man when he comes back to dazzle his native town. The children of the working people learn many useful things in the public schools, but the commercial arithmetic, and many other studies, are founded on the tacit assumption that a boy rises in life by getting away from manual labor, — that every promising boy goes into business or a profession. The children destined for factory life are furnished with what would be most useful under other conditions, quite as the prosperous farmer's wife buys a folding-bed for her huge four-cornered "spare room," because her sister, who has married a city man, is obliged to have a folding-bed in the cramped limits of her flat. Partly because so little is done for him educationally, and partly because he must live narrowly and dress meanly, the life of the average laborer tends to become flat and monotonous, with nothing in his work to feed his mind or hold his interest. Theoretically, we would all admit that the man at the bottom, who performs the meanest and humblest work, so long as the work is necessary, performs a useful function; but we do not live up to our theories, and in addition to his hard and uninteresting work he is covered with a sort of contempt, and unless he falls into illness or trouble, he receives little sympathy or attention. Certainly no serious effort is made to give him a participation in the social and industrial life with which he comes in contact, nor any insight and inspiration regarding it.

Apparently we have not yet recovered manual labor from the deep distrust which centuries of slavery and the feudal system have cast upon it. To get away from menial work, to do obviously little with one's hands, is still the desirable status. This may readily be seen all along the line. A workingman's family will make every effort and

sacrifice that the brightest daughter be sent
to the high school and through the normal
school, quite as much because a teacher in
the family raises the general social standing
and sense of family consequence, as that the
returns are superior to factory or even office
work. "Teacher" in the vocabulary of many
children is a synonym for women-folk gentry,
and the name is indiscriminately applied to
women of certain dress and manner. The
same desire for social advancement is expressed by the purchasing of a piano, or the
fact that the son is an office boy, and not a
factory hand. The overcrowding of the pro-
fessions by poorly equipped men arises from
much the same source, and from the conviction that, "an education" is wasted if a boy
goes into a factory or shop.

A Chicago manufacturer tells a story of
twin boys, whom he befriended and meant
to give a start in life. He sent them both
to the Athenæum for several winters as a
preparatory business training, and then took
them into his office, where they speedily

became known as the bright one and the stupid one. The stupid one was finally dismissed after repeated trials, when to the surprise of the entire establishment, he quickly betook himself into the shops, where he became a wide-awake and valuable workman. His chagrined benefactor, in telling the story, admits that he himself had fallen a victim to his own business training and his early notion of rising in life. In reality he had merely followed the lead of most benevolent people who help poor boys. They test the success of their efforts by the number whom they have taken out of factory work into some other and "higher occupation."

Quite in line with this commercial ideal are the night schools and institutions of learning most accessible to working people. First among them is the business college which teaches largely the mechanism of type-writing and book-keeping, and lays all stress upon commerce and methods of distribution. Commodities are treated as exports and imports, or solely in regard to their commercial value, and not, of course, in relation to their historic development or the manufacturing processes to which they have been subjected. These schools do not in the least minister to the needs of the actual factory employee, who is in the shop and not in the office. We assume that all men are searching for "puddings and power," to use Carlyle's phrase, and furnish only the schools which help them to those ends.

The business college man, or even the man who goes through an academic course in order to prepare for a profession, comes to look on learning too much as an investment from which he will later reap the benefits in earning money. He does not connect learning with industrial pursuits, nor does he in the least lighten or illuminate those pursuits for those of his friends who have not risen in life. "It is as though nets were laid at the entrance to education, in which those who by some means or other escape from the masses bowed down by labor, are inevitably caught and held from substantial service to their fellows." The academic teaching which is accessible to workingmen through University Extension lectures and classes at settlements, is usually bookish and remote, and concerning subjects completely divorced from their actual experiences. The men come to think of learning as something to be added to the end of a hard day's work, and to be gained at the cost of toilsome mental exertion. There are, of course, exceptions, but many men who persist in attending classes and lectures year after year find themselves possessed of a mass of inert knowledge which nothing in their experience fuses into availability or realization.

Among the many disappointments which the settlement experiment has brought to its promoters, perhaps none is keener than the fact that they have as yet failed to work out methods of education, specialized

and adapted to the needs of adult working
people in contra-distinction to those employed in schools and colleges, or those
used in teaching children. There are
many excellent reasons and explanations
for this failure. In the first place, the
residents themselves are for the most part
imbued with academic methods and ideals,
which it is most difficult to modify. To
quote from a late settlement report, " The
most vaunted educational work in settlements amounts often to the stimulation
mentally of a select few who are, in a
sense, of the academic type of mind, and
who easily and quickly respond to the
academic methods employed." These classes
may be valuable, but they leave quite
untouched the great mass of the factory
population, the ordinary workingman of
the ordinary workingman's street, whose
attitude is best described as that of "ac-
quiescence," who lives through the aimless passage of the years without incentive
" to imagine, to design, or to aspire."

These men are totally untouched by all the educational and philanthropic machinery which is designed for the young and the helpless who live on the same streets with them. They do not often drink to excess, they regularly give all their wages to their wives, they have a vague pride in their superior children; but they grow prematurely old and stiff in all their muscles, and become more and more taciturn, their entire energies consumed in "holding a job."

Various attempts have been made to break through the inadequate educational facilities supplied by commercialism and scholarship, both of which have followed their own ideals and have failed to look at the situation as it actually presents itself. The most noteworthy attempt has been the movement toward industrial education, the agitation for which has been ably seconded by manufacturers of a practical type, who have from time to time founded and endowed technical schools, designed for workingmen's sons. The early schools of this type inevitably reflected the ideal of the self-made man. They succeeded in transferring a few skilled workers into the upper class of trained engineers, and a few less skilled workers into the class of trained mechanics, but did not aim to educate the many who are doomed to the unskilled work which the permanent specialization of the division of labor demands.

The Peter Coopers and other good men honestly believed that if intelligence could be added to industry, each workingman who faithfully attended these schools could walk into increased skill and wages, and in time even become an employer himself. Such schools are useful beyond doubt; but so far as educating workingmen is concerned or in any measure satisfying the democratic ideal, they plainly beg the question.

Almost every large city has two or three polytechnic institutions founded by rich men, anxious to help "poor boys." These have been captured by conventional educators for the purpose of fitting young men for the colleges and universities. They have compromised by merely adding to the usual academic course manual work, applied mathematics, mechanical drawing and engineering. Two schools in Chicago, plainly founded for the sons of workingmen, afford an illustration of this tendency and result. On the other hand, so far as schools of this type have been captured by commercialism, they turn out trained engineers, professional chemists, and electricians. They are polytechnics of a high order, but do not even pretend to admit the workingman with his meagre intellectual equipment. They graduate machine builders, but not educated machine tenders. Even the textile schools are largely seized by young men who expect to be superintendents of factories, designers, or manufacturers themselves, and the textile worker who actually "holds the thread" is seldom seen in them; indeed, in one of the largest schools women are not allowed, in spite of the fact that spinning and weaving have traditionally been woman's work, and that thousands of women are at present employed in the textile mills.

It is much easier to go over the old paths of education with "manual training" thrown in, as it were; it is much simpler to appeal to the old ambitions of "getting on in life," or of "preparing for a profession," or "for a commercial career," than to work out new methods on democratic lines. These schools gradually drop back into the conventional courses, modified in some slight degree, while the adaptation to working-men's needs is never made, nor, indeed, vigorously attempted. In the meantime, the manufacturers continually protest that engineers, especially trained for devising machines, are not satisfactory. Three generations of workers have invented, but we are told that invention no longer goes on in the workshop, even when it is artificially stimulated by the offer of prizes, and that the inventions of the last quarter of the nineteenth century have by no means fulfilled the promise of the earlier three-quarters.

Every foreman in a large factory has had experience with two classes of men: first with those who become rigid and tolerate no change in their work, partly because they make more money "working by the piece," when they stick to that work which they have learned to do rapidly, and partly because the entire muscular and nervous system has become by daily use adapted to particular motions and resents change. Secondly, there are the men who float in and out of the factory, in a constantly changing stream. They "quit work" for the slightest reason or none at all, and never become skilled at anything. Some of them are men of low intelligence, but many of them are merely too nervous and restless, too impatient, too easily "driven to drink," to be of any use in a modern factory. They are the men for whom the demanded adaptation is impossible.

The individual from whom the industrial

order demands ever larger drafts of time and energy, should be nourished and enriched from social sources, in proportion as he is drained. He, more than other men, needs the conception of historic continuity in order to reveal to him the purpose and utility of his work, and he can only be stimulated and dignified as he obtains a conception of his proper relation to society. Scholarship is evidently unable to do this for him; for, unfortunately, the same tendency to division of labor has also produced over-specialization in scholarship, with the sad result that when the scholar attempts to minister to a worker, he gives him the result of more specialization rather than an offset from it. He cannot bring healing and solace because he himself is suffering from the same disease. There is indeed a deplorable lack of perception and adaptation on the part of educators all along the line.

It will certainly be embarrassing to have our age written down triumphant in the matter of inventions, in that our factories

were filled with intricate machines, the result
of advancing mathematical and mechanical
knowledge in relation to manufacturing processes, but defeated in that it lost its head
over the achievement and forgot the men.
The accusation would stand, that the age
failed to perform a like service in the extension of history and art to the factory
employees who ran the machines; that the
machine tenders, heavy and almost dehuman-
ized by monotonous toil, walked about in
the same streets with us, and sat in the same
cars; but that we were absolutely indifferent
and made no genuine effort to supply to them
the artist's perception or student's insight,
which alone could fuse them into social consciousness. It would further stand that the
scholars among us continued with yet more
research, that the educators were concerned
only with the young and the promising, and
the philanthropists with the criminals and
helpless.

There is a pitiful failure to recognize the
situation in which the majority of working

people are placed, a tendency to ignore their real experiences and needs, and, most stupid of all, we leave quite untouched affections and memories which would afford a tremendous dynamic if they were utilized.

We constantly hear it said in educational circles, that a child learns only by "doing," and that education must proceed "through the eyes and hands to the brain"; and yet for the vast number of people all around us who do not need to have activities artificially provided, and who use their hands and eyes all the time, we do not seem able to reverse the process. We quote the dictum, "What is learned in the schoolroom must be applied in the workshop," and yet the skill and handicraft constantly used in the workshop have no relevance or meaning given to them by the school; and when we do try to help the workingman in an educational way, we completely ignore his everyday occupation. Yet the task is merely one of adaptation. It is to take actual conditions and to make them the basis for a large and generous method of education, to perform a difficult idealization doubtless, but not an impossible one.

We apparently believe that the working-man has no chance to realize life through his vocation. We easily recognize the historic association in regard to ancient buildings. We say that "generation after generation have stamped their mark upon them, have recorded their thoughts in them, until they have become the property of all." And yet this is even more true of the instruments of labor, which have constantly been held in human hands. A machine really represents the "seasoned life of man" preserved and treasured up within itself, quite as much as an ancient building does. At present, work-men are brought in contact with the machinery with which they work as abruptly as if the present set of industrial implements had been newly created. They handle the machinery day by day, without any notion of its gradual evolution and growth. Few of the men who perform the mechanical work

in the great factories have any comprehension
of the fact that the inventions upon which
the factory depends, the instruments which
they use, have been slowly worked out, each
generation using the gifts of the last and
transmitting the inheritance until it has become a social possession. This can only be
understood by a man who has obtained some
idea of social progress. We are still child-
ishly pleased when we see the further subdivision of labor going on, because the
quantity of the output is increased thereby,
and we apparently are unable to take our
attention away from the product long enough
to really focus it upon the producer. Theoretically, " the division of labor " makes men
more interdependent and human by drawing them together into a unity of purpose.
" If a number of people decide to build a
road, and one digs, and one brings stones,
and another breaks them, they are quite
inevitably united by their interest in the
road. But this naturally presupposes that
they know where the road is going to, that

they have some curiosity and interest about it, and perhaps a chance to travel upon it." If the division of labor robs them of interest in any part of it, the mere mechanical fact of interdependence amounts to nothing.

The man in the factory, as well as the man with the hoe, has a grievance beyond being overworked and disinherited, in that he does not know what it is all about. We may well regret the passing of the time when the variety of work performed in the unspecialized workshop naturally stimulated the intelligence of the workingmen and brought them into contact both with the raw material and the finished product. But the problem of education, as any advanced educator will tell us, is to supply the essentials of experience by a short cut, as it were. If the shop constantly tends to make the workman a specialist, then the problem of the educator in regard to him is quite clear: it is to give him what may be an offset from the over-specialization of his daily work, to supply him with general information and to insist that he shall be a cultivated member of society with a consciousness of his industrial and social value.

As sad a sight as an old hand-loom worker in a factory attempting to make his clumsy machine compete with the flying shuttles about him, is a workingman equipped with knowledge so meagre that he can get no meaning into his life nor sequence between his acts and the far-off results.

Manufacturers, as a whole, however, when they attempt educational institutions in connection with their factories, are prone to follow conventional lines, and to exhibit the weakness of imitation. We find, indeed, that the middle-class educator constantly makes the mistakes of the middle-class moralist when he attempts to aid working people. The latter has constantly and traditionally urged upon the workingman the specialized virtues of thrift, industry, and sobriety — all virtues pertaining to the individual. When each man had his own shop, it was perhaps wise to lay almost

exclusive stress upon the industrial virtues
of diligence and thrift; but as industry
has become more highly organized, life becomes incredibly complex and interdependent. If a workingman is to have a conception of his value at all, he must see
industry in its unity and entirety; he must
have a conception that will include not
only himself and his immediate family and
community, but the industrial organization
as a whole. It is doubtless true that dex-
terity of hand becomes less and less imper-
ative as the invention of machinery and
subdivision of labor proceeds; but it becomes all the more necessary, if the workman is to save his life at all, that he
should get a sense of his individual relation to the system. Feeding a machine
with a material of which he has no knowledge, producing a product, totally unrelated
to the rest of his life, without in the least
knowing what becomes of it, or its connection with the community, is, of course, un-
questionably deadening to his intellectual

DEMOCRACY AND SOCIAL ETHICS

and moral life. To make the moral connection it would be necessary to give him a social consciousness of the value of his work, and
at least a sense of participation and a certain
joy in its ultimate use; to make the intellectual connection it would be essential to
create in him some historic conception of
the development of industry and the relation
of his individual work to it.

Workingmen themselves have made attempts in both directions, which it would
be well for moralists and educators to
study. It is a striking fact that when
workingmen formulate their own moral
code, and try to inspire and encourage
each other, it is always a large and general doctrine which they preach. They
were the first class of men to organize an
international association, and the constant
talk at a modern labor meeting is of soli-
darity and of the identity of the interests
of workingmen the world over. It is difficult to secure a successful organization of
men into the simplest trades organization

without an appeal to the most abstract
principles of justice and brotherhood. As
they have formulated their own morals by
laying the greatest stress upon the largest
morality, so if they could found their own
schools, it is doubtful whether they would
be of the mechanic institute type. Courses
of study arranged by a group of workingmen are most naïve in their breadth and
generality. They will select the history of
the world in preference to that of any
period or nation. The "wonders of science" or "the story of evolution" will
attract workingmen to a lecture when zoöl-
ogy or chemistry will drive them away.
The "outlines of literature" or "the best
in literature" will draw an audience when
a lecturer in English poetry will be solitary.
This results partly from a wholesome desire
to have general knowledge before special
knowledge, and is partly a rebound from
the specialization of labor to which the
workingman is subjected. When he is
free from work and can direct his own

mind, he tends to roam, to dwell upon large themes. Much the same tendency is found in programmes of study arranged by Woman's Clubs in country places. The untrained mind, wearied with meaningless detail, when it gets an opportunity to make its demand heard, asks for general philosophy and background.

In a certain sense commercialism itself, at least in its larger aspect, tends to educate the workingman better than organized education does. Its interests are certainly world-wide and democratic, while it is absolutely undiscriminating as to country and creed, coming into contact with all climes and races. If this aspect of commercialism were utilized, it would in a measure counter-balance the tendency which results from the subdivision of labor.

The most noteworthy attempt to utilize this democracy of commerce in relation to manufacturing is found at Dayton, Ohio, in the yearly gatherings held in a large factory there. Once a year the entire force is gathered together to hear the returns of the business, not so much in respect to the profits, as in regard to its extension. At these meetings, the travelling salesmen from various parts of the world — from Constantinople, from Berlin, from Rome, from Hong Kong — report upon the sales they have made, and the methods of advertisement and promotion adapted to the various countries.

Stereopticon lectures are given upon each new country as soon as it has been successfully invaded by the product of the factory. The foremen in the various departments of the factory give accounts of the increased efficiency and the larger output over former years. Any man who has made an invention in connection with the machinery of the factory, at this time publicly receives a prize, and suggestions are approved that tend to increase the comfort and social facilities of the employees. At least for the moment there is a complete esprit de corps, and the youngest and least skilled employee sees himself in connection with the interests of the firm, and the spread of an invention. It is a crude example of what might be done in the way of giving a large framework of meaning to factory labor, and of putting it into a sentient background, at least on the commercial side.

It is easy to indict the educator, to say that he has gotten entangled in his own material, and has fallen a victim to his own methods; but granting this, what has the artist done about it — he who is supposed to have a more intimate insight into the needs of his contemporaries, and to minister to them as none other can?

It is quite true that a few writers are insisting that the growing desire for labor, on the part of many people of leisure, has its counterpart in the increasing desire for general knowledge on the part of many laborers. They point to the fact that the same duality of conscience which seems to stifle the noblest effort in the individual because his intellectual conception and his achievement are so difficult to bring together, is found on a large scale in society itself, when we have the separation of the people who think from those who work. And yet, since Ruskin ceased, no one has really formulated this in a convincing form. And even Ruskin's famous dictum, that labor without art brutalizes, has always been interpreted as if art could only be a sense of beauty or joy in one's own work, and not a sense of companionship with all other workers. The situation demands the consciousness of participation and well-being which comes to the individual when he is able to see himself "in connection and co-operation with the whole"; it needs the solace of collective art inherent in collective labor.

As the poet bathes the outer world for us in the hues of human feeling, so the workman needs some one to bathe his surroundings with a human significance — some one who shall teach him to find that which will give a potency to his life. His education, however simple, should tend to make him widely at home in the world, and to give him a sense of simplicity and peace in the midst of the triviality and noise to which he is constantly subjected. He, like other men, can learn to be content to see but a part, although it must be a part of something.

It is because of a lack of democracy that we do not really incorporate him in the hopes and advantages of society, and give him the place which is his by simple right. We have learned to say that the good must be extended to all of society before it can be held secure by any one person or any one class; but we have not yet learned to add to that statement, that unless all men and all classes contribute to a good, we cannot even be sure that it is worth having. In spite of many attempts we do not really act upon either statement.

CHAPTER VII

Political Reform

THROUGHOUT this volume we have assumed that much of our ethical maladjustment in social affairs arises from the fact that we are acting upon a code of ethics adapted to individual relationships, but not to the larger social relationships to which it is bunglingly applied. In addition, however, to the consequent strain and difficulty, there is often an honest lack of perception as to what the situation demands.

Nowhere is this more obvious than in our political life as it manifests itself in certain quarters of every great city. It is most difficult to hold to our political democracy and to make it in any sense a social expression and not a mere governmental contrivance, unless we take pains to keep on common ground in our human experiences. Otherwise there is in various parts of the community an inevitable difference of ethical standards which becomes responsible for much misunderstanding.

It is difficult both to interpret sympathetically the motives and ideals of those who have acquired rules of conduct in experience widely different from our own, and also to take enough care in guarding the gains already made, and in valuing highly enough the imperfect good so painfully acquired and, at the best, so mixed with evil. This wide difference in daily experience exhibits itself in two distinct attitudes toward politics. The well-to-do men of the community think of politics as something off by itself; they may conscientiously recognize political duty as part of good citizenship, but political effort is not the expression of their moral or social life. As a result of this detachment, "reform movements," started by business men and the better element, are almost wholly occupied in the correction of political machinery and with a concern for the better method of administration, rather than with the ultimate purpose of securing the welfare of the people. They fix their attention so exclusively on methods that they fail to consider the final aims of city government. This accounts for the growing tendency to put more and more responsibility upon executive officers and appointed commissions at the expense of curtailing the power of the direct representatives of the voters. Reform movements tend to become negative and to lose their educational value for the mass of the people. The reformers take the rôle of the opposition. They give themselves largely to criticisms of the present state of affairs, to writing and talking of what the future must be and of certain results which should be obtained. In trying to better matters, however, they have in mind only political achievements which they detach in a curious way from the rest of life, and they speak and write of the purification of politics as of a thing set apart from daily life.

On the other hand, the real leaders of the people are part of the entire life of the community which they control, and so far as they are representative at all, are giving a social expression to democracy. They are often politically corrupt, but in spite of this they are proceeding upon a sounder theory. Although they would be totally unable to give it abstract expression, they are really acting upon a formulation made by a shrewd English observer; namely, that, "after the enfranchisement of the masses, social ideals enter into political programmes, and they enter not as something which at best can be indirectly promoted by government, but as something which it is the chief business of government to advance directly."

Men living near to the masses of voters, and knowing them intimately, recognize this and act upon it; they minister directly to life and to social needs. They realize that the people as a whole are clamoring for social results, and they hold their power because they respond to that demand. They are corrupt and often do their work badly; but they at least avoid the mistake of a certain type of business men who are frightened by democracy, and have lost their faith in the people. The two standards are similar to those seen at a popular exhibition of pictures where the cultivated people care most for the technique of a given painting, the moving mass for a subject that shall be domestic and human.

This difference may be illustrated by the writer's experience in a certain ward of Chicago, during three campaigns, when efforts were made to dislodge an alderman who had represented the ward for many years. In this ward there are gathered together fifty thousand people, representing a score of nationalities; the newly emigrated Latin, Teuton, Celt, Greek, and Slav who live there have little in common save the basic experiences which come to men in all countries and under all conditions. In order to make fifty thousand people, so heterogeneous in nationality, religion, and customs, agree upon any demand, it must be founded upon universal experiences which are perforce individual and not social.

An instinctive recognition of this on the part of the alderman makes it possible to understand the individualistic basis of his political success, but it remains extremely difficult to ascertain the reasons for the extreme leniency of judgment concerning the political corruption of which he is constantly guilty.

This leniency is only to be explained on the ground that his constituents greatly admire individual virtues, and that they are at the same time unable to perceive social outrages which the alderman may be committing. They thus free the alderman from blame because his corruption is social, and they honestly admire him as a great man and hero, because his individual acts are on the whole kindly and generous.

In certain stages of moral evolution, a man is incapable of action unless the results will benefit himself or some one of his acquaintances, and it is a long step in moral progress to set the good of the many before the interest of the few, and to be concerned for the welfare of a community without hope of an individual return. How far the selfish politician befools his constituents into believing that their interests are identical with his own; how far he presumes upon their inability to distinguish between the individual and social virtues, an inability which he himself shares with them; and how far he dazzles them by the sense of his greatness, and a conviction that they participate therein, it is difficult to determine.

Morality certainly develops far earlier in the form of moral fact than in the form of moral ideas, and it is obvious that ideas only operate upon the popular mind through will and character, and must be dramatized before they reach the mass of men, even as the biography of the saints have been after all "the main guide to the stumbling feet of thousands of Christians to whom the Credo has been but mysterious words."

Ethics as well as political opinions may be discussed and disseminated among the sophisticated by lectures and printed pages, but to the common people they can only come through example — through a personality which seizes the popular imagination. The advantage of an unsophisticated neighborhood is, that the inhabitants do not keep their ideas as treasures — they are untouched by the notion of accumulating them, as they might knowledge or money, and they frankly act upon those they have. The personal example promptly rouses to emulation. In a neighborhood where political standards are plastic and undeveloped, and where there has been little previous experience in self-government, the office-holder himself sets the standard, and the ideas that cluster around him exercise a specific and permanent influence upon the political morality of his constituents.

Nothing is more certain than that the quality which a heterogeneous population, living in one of the less sophisticated wards,

most admires is the quality of simple goodness; that the man who attracts them is the
one whom they believe to be a good man.
We all know that children long "to be
good" with an intensity which they give to
no other ambition. We can all remember
that the earliest strivings of our childhood
were in this direction, and that we vener-
ated grown people because they had attained
perfection.

Primitive people, such as the South Italian
peasants, are still in this stage. They want
to be good, and deep down in their hearts
they admire nothing so much as the good
man. Abstract virtues are too difficult for
their untrained minds to apprehend, and
many of them are still simple enough to
believe that power and wealth come only to
good people.

The successful candidate, then, must be a
good man according to the morality of his
constituents. He must not attempt to hold
up too high a standard, nor must he attempt
to reform or change their standards. His

safety lies in doing on a large scale the good
deeds which his constituents are able to do
only on a small scale. If he believes what
they believe and does what they are all
cherishing a secret ambition to do, he will
dazzle them by his success and win their
confidence. There is a certain wisdom in
this course. There is a common sense in
the mass of men which cannot be neglected
with impunity, just as there is sure to be
an eccentricity in the differing and reforming individual which it is perhaps well to
challenge.

The constant kindness of the poor to each
other was pointed out in a previous chapter,
and that they unfailingly respond to the need
and distresses of their poorer neighbors even
when in danger of bankruptcy themselves.
The kindness which a poor man shows his
distressed neighbor is doubtless heightened
by the consciousness that he himself may be
in distress next week; he therefore stands
by his friend when he gets too drunk to take
care of himself, when he loses his wife or

child, when he is evicted for non-payment of rent, when he is arrested for a petty crime. It seems to such a man entirely fitting that his alderman should do the same thing on a larger scale — that he should help a constituent out of trouble, merely because he is in trouble, irrespective of the justice involved.

The alderman therefore bails out his constituents when they are arrested, or says a good word to the police justice when they appear before him for trial, uses his pull with the magistrate when they are likely to be fined for a civil misdemeanor, or sees what he can do to "fix up matters" with the state's attorney when the charge is really a serious one, and in doing this he follows the ethics held and practised by his constituents. All this conveys the impression to the simple-minded that law is not enforced, if the lawbreaker have a powerful friend. One may instance the alderman's action in standing by an Italian padrone of the ward when he was indicted for violating the civil service regulations. The commissioners had sent out notices to certain Italian day-laborers who were upon the eligible list that they were to report for work at a given day and hour. One of the padrones intercepted these notifications and sold them to the men for five dollars apiece, making also the usual bargain for a share of their wages. The padrone's entire arrangement followed the custom which had prevailed for years before the establishment of civil service laws. Ten of the laborers swore out warrants against the padrone, who was convicted and fined seventy-five dollars. This sum was promptly paid by the alderman, and the padrone, assured that he would be protected from any further trouble, returned uninjured to the colony. The simple Italians were much bewildered by this show of a power stronger than that of the civil service, which they had trusted as they did the one in Italy. The first violation of its authority was made, and various sinister acts have followed, until no Italian who is digging a sewer or sweeping a street for the city feels quite secure in holding his

job unless he is backed by the friendship of
the alderman. According to the civil service law, a laborer has no right to a trial;
many are discharged by the foreman, and
find that they can be reinstated only upon
the aldermanic recommendation. He thus
practically holds his old power over the
laborers working for the city. The popular
mind is convinced that an honest administration of civil service is impossible, and that
it is but one more instrument in the hands
of the powerful.

It will be difficult to establish genuine
civil service among these men, who learn
only by experience, since their experiences
have been of such a nature that their unani-
mous vote would certainly be that "civil
service" is "no good."

As many of his constituents in this case
are impressed with the fact that the aldermanic power is superior to that of government, so instances of actual lawbreaking
might easily be cited. A young man may
enter a saloon long after midnight, the legal

closing hour, and seat himself at a gambling table, perfectly secure from interruption or arrest, because the place belongs to an alderman; but in order to secure this immunity the policeman on the beat must pretend not to see into the windows each time that he passes, and he knows, and the young man knows that he knows, that nothing would embarrass "Headquarters" more than to have an arrest made on those premises. A certain contempt for the whole machinery of law and order is thus easily fostered.

Because of simple friendliness the alderman is expected to pay rent for the hard-pressed tenant when no rent is forthcoming, to find "jobs" when work is hard to get, to procure and divide among his constituents all the places which he can seize from the city hall. The alderman of the ward we are considering at one time could make the proud boast that he had twenty-six hundred people in his ward upon the public pay-roll. This, of course, included day laborers, but each one felt under distinct obligations to him for getting a position. When we reflect that this is one-third of the entire vote of the ward, we realize that it is very important to vote for the right man, since there is, at the least, one chance out of three for securing work.

If we recollect further that the franchise-seeking companies pay respectful heed to the applicants backed by the alderman, the question of voting for the successful man becomes as much an industrial one as a political one. An Italian laborer wants a "job" more than anything else, and quite simply votes for the man who promises him one. It is not so different from his relation to the padrone, and, indeed, the two strengthen each other.

The alderman may himself be quite sincere in his acts of kindness, for an office seeker may begin with the simple desire to alleviate suffering, and this may gradually change into the desire to put his constituents under obligations to him; but the action of such an individual becomes a demoralizing element in the community when kindly impulse is made a cloak for the satisfaction of personal ambition, and when the plastic morals of his constituents gradually conform to his own undeveloped standards.

The alderman gives presents at weddings and christenings. He seizes these days of family festivities for making friends. It is easiest to reach them in the holiday mood of expansive good-will, but on their side it seems natural and kindly that he should do it. The alderman procures passes from the railroads when his constituents wish to visit friends or attend the funerals of distant relatives; he buys tickets galore for benefit entertainments given for a widow or a consumptive in peculiar distress; he contributes to prizes which are awarded to the handsomest lady or the most popular man. At a church bazaar, for instance, the alderman finds the stage all set for his dramatic performance. When others

are spending pennies, he is spending dol·
lars. When anxious relatives are canvass-
ing to secure votes for the two most
beautiful children who are being voted
upon, he recklessly buys votes from both
sides, and laughingly declines to say which
one he likes best, buying off the young
lady who is persistently determined to find
out, with five dollars for the flower bazaar,
the posies, of course, to be sent to the sick
of the parish. The moral atmosphere of a
bazaar suits him exactly. He murmurs
many times, "Never mind, the money all
goes to the poor; it is all straight enough
if the church gets it, the poor won't ask
too many questions." The oftener he can
put such sentiments into the minds of his
constituents, the better he is pleased. Nothing so rapidly prepares them to take his
view of money getting and money spending. We see again the process disregarded,
because the end itself is considered so praiseworthy.

There is something archaic in a com-

munity of simple people in their attitude
toward death and burial. There is nothing so easy to collect money for as a
funeral, and one involuntarily remembers
that the early religious tithes were paid to
ward off death and ghosts. At times one
encounters almost the Greek feeling in regard to burial. If the alderman seizes
upon times of festivities for expressions of
his good-will, much more does he seize
upon periods of sorrow. At a funeral he
has the double advantage of ministering
to a genuine craving for comfort and solace, and at the same time of assisting a
bereaved constituent to express that curious
feeling of remorse, which is ever an accom-
paniment of quick sorrow, that desire to
"make up" for past delinquencies, to show
the world how much he loved the person
who has just died, which is as natural as
it is universal.

In addition to this, there is, among the
poor, who have few social occasions, a
great desire for a well-arranged funeral, the

grade of which almost determines their social standing in the neighborhood. The alderman saves the very poorest of his constituents from that awful horror of burial by the county; he provides carriages for the poor, who otherwise could not have them. It may be too much to say that all the relatives and friends who ride in the carriages provided by the alderman's bounty vote for him, but they are certainly influenced by his kindness, and talk of his virtues during the long hours of the ride back and forth from the suburban cemetery. A man who would ask at such a time where all the money thus spent comes from would be considered sinister. The tendency to speak lightly of the faults of the dead and to judge them gently is transferred to the living, and many a man at such a time has formulated a lenient judgment of political corruption, and has heard kindly speeches which he has remembered on election day. " Ah, well, he has a big Irish heart. He is good to the widow and the fatherless." "He knows the poor better than the big guns who are always talking about civil service and reform."

Indeed, what headway can the notion of civic purity, of honesty of administration make against this big manifestation of human friendliness, this stalking survival of village kindness? The notions of the civic reformer are negative and impotent before it. Such an alderman will keep a standing account with an undertaker, and telephone every week, and sometimes more than once, the kind of funeral he wishes provided for a bereaved constituent, until the sum may roll up into "hundreds a year." He understands what the people want, and ministers just as truly to a great human need as the musician or the artist. An attempt to substitute what we might call a later standard was made at one time when a delicate little child was deserted in the Hull-House nursery. An investigation showed that it had been born ten days previously in the

Cook County hospital, but no trace could be found of the unfortunate mother. The little child lived for several weeks, and then, in spite of every care, died. It was decided to have it buried by the county authorities, and the wagon was to arrive at eleven o'clock; about nine o'clock in the morning the rumor of this awful deed reached the neighbors. A half dozen of them came, in a very excited state of mind, to protest. They took up a collection out of their poverty with which to defray a funeral. The residents of Hull-House were then comparatively new in the neighborhood and did not realize that they were really shocking a genuine moral sentiment of the community. In their crudeness they instanced the care and tenderness which had been expended upon the little creature while it was alive; that it had had every attention from a skilled physician and a trained nurse, and even intimated that the excited members of the group had not taken part in this, and that it now lay with the nursery to decide that it should be buried as

it had been born, at the county's expense.
It is doubtful if Hull-House has ever done
anything which injured it so deeply in the
minds of some of its neighbors. It was
only forgiven by the most indulgent on the
ground that the residents were spinsters, and
could not know a mother's heart. No one
born and reared in the community could
possibly have made a mistake like that. No
one who had studied the ethical standards
with any care could have bungled so
completely.

We are constantly underestimating the
amount of sentiment among simple people.
The songs which are most popular among
them are those of a reminiscent old age, in
which the ripened soul calmly recounts and
regrets the sins of his youth, songs in
which the wayward daughter is forgiven
by her loving parents, in which the lovers
are magnanimous and faithful through all
vicissitudes. The tendency is to condone
and forgive, and not hold too rigidly to a
standard. In the theatres it is the magnani-

mous man, the kindly reckless villain who is always applauded. So shrewd an observer as Samuel Johnson once remarked that it was surprising to find how much more kindness than justice society contained.

On the same basis the alderman manages several saloons, one down town within easy access of the city hall, where he can catch the more important of his friends. Here again he has seized upon an old tradition and primitive custom, the good fellowship which has long been best expressed when men drink together. The saloons offer a common meeting ground, with stimulus enough to free the wits and tongues of the men who meet there.

He distributes each Christmas many tons of turkeys not only to voters, but to families who are represented by no vote. By a judicious management some families get three or four turkeys apiece; but what of that, the alderman has none of the nagging rules of the charitable societies, nor does he declare that because a man wants two turkeys for Christmas, he is a scoundrel who shall never be allowed to eat turkey again. As he does not distribute his Christmas favors from any hardly acquired philanthropic motive, there is no disposition to apply the carefully evolved rules of the charitable societies to his beneficiaries. Of course, there are those who suspect that the benevolence rests upon self-seeking motives, and feel themselves quite freed from any sense of gratitude; others go further and glory in the fact that they can thus " soak the alderman." An example of this is the young man who fills his pockets with a handful of cigars, giving a sly wink at the others. But this freedom from any sense of obligation is often the first step downward to the position where he is willing to sell his vote to both parties, and then scratch his ticket as he pleases. The writer recalls a conversation with a man in which he complained quite openly, and with no sense of shame, that his vote had " sold for only two dollars this year," and that he was " awfully disappointed." The writer happened to know that his income during the nine months previous had been but twenty-eight dollars, and that he was in debt thirty-two dollars, and she could well imagine the eagerness with which he had counted upon this source of revenue. After some years the selling of votes becomes a commonplace, and but little attempt is made upon the part of the buyer or seller to conceal the fact, if the transaction runs smoothly.

A certain lodging-house keeper at one time sold the votes of his entire house to a political party and was " well paid for it too"; but being of a grasping turn, he also sold the house for the same election to the rival party. Such an outrage could not be borne. The man was treated to a modern version of tar and feathers, and as a result of being held under a street hydrant in November, contracted pneumonia which resulted in his death. No official investigation took place, since the doctor's certificate of pneumonia was sufficient for legal burial, and public sentiment sustained the action. In various conversations which the writer had concerning the entire transaction, she discovered great indignation concerning his duplicity and treachery, but none whatever for his original offence of selling out the votes of his house.

A club will be started for the express purpose of gaining a reputation for political power which may later be sold out. The president and executive committee of such a club, who will naturally receive the funds, promise to divide with "the boys" who swell the size of the membership. A reform movement is at first filled with recruits who are active and loud in their assertions of the number of votes they can "deliver." The reformers are delighted with this display of zeal, and only gradually find out that many of the recruits are there for the express purpose of being bought by the other side; that they are most active in order to seem valuable, and thus raise the price of their allegiance when they are ready to sell. Reformers seeing them drop away one by one, talk of desertion from the ranks of reform, and of the power of money over well-meaning men, who are too weak to withstand temptation; but in reality the men are not deserters because they have never actually been enrolled in the ranks. The money they take is neither a bribe nor the price of their loyalty, it is simply the consummation of a long-cherished plan and a well-earned reward. They came into the new movement for the purpose of being bought out of it, and have successfully accomplished that purpose.

Hull-House assisted in carrying on two unsuccessful campaigns against the same alderman. In the two years following the end of the first one, nearly every man who had been prominent in it had received an office from the reëlected alderman. A printer had been appointed to a clerkship in the city hall; a driver received a large salary for services in the police barns; the candidate himself, a bricklayer, held a position in the city construction department. At the beginning of the next campaign, the greatest difficulty was experienced in finding a candidate, and each one proposed, demanded time to consider the proposition. During this period he invariably became the recipient of the alderman's bounty. The first one, who was foreman of a large factory, was reported to have been bought off by the promise that the city institutions would use the product of his firm. The second one, a keeper of a grocery and family saloon, with large popularity, was promised the aldermanic nomination on the regular ticket at the expiration of the term of office held by the alderman's colleague, and it may be well to state in passing that he was thus nominated and successfully elected. The third proposed candidate received a place for his son in the office of the city attorney.

Not only are offices in his gift, but all smaller favors as well. Any requests to the council, or special licenses, must be presented by the alderman of the ward in which the person desiring the favor resides.

There is thus constant opportunity for the alderman to put his constituents under obligations to him, to make it difficult for a constituent to withstand him, or for one with large interests to enter into political action at all. From the Italian pedler who wants a license to peddle fruit in the street, to the large manufacturing company who desires to tunnel an alley for the sake of conveying pipes from one building to another, everybody is under obligations to his alderman, and is constantly made to feel it. In short, these very regulations for presenting requests to the council have been made, by the aldermen themselves, for the express purpose of increasing the dependence of their constituents, and thereby augmenting aldermanic power and prestige.

The alderman has also a very singular hold upon the property owners of his ward. The paving, both of the streets and sidewalks throughout his district, is disgraceful; and in the election speeches the reform side holds him responsible for this condition, and promises better paving under another régime. But the paving could not be made better without a special assessment upon the property owners of the vicinity, and paying more taxes is exactly what his constituents do not want to do. In reality, "getting them off," or at the worst postponing the time of the improvement, is one of the genuine favors which he performs. A movement to have the paving done from a general fund would doubtless be opposed by the property owners in other parts of the city who have already paid for the asphalt bordering their own possessions, but they have no conception of the struggle and possible bankruptcy which repaving may mean to the small property owner, nor how his chief concern may be to elect an alderman who cares more for the feelings and pocket-books of his constituents than he does for the repute and cleanliness of his city.

The alderman exhibited great wisdom in procuring from certain of his down-town friends the sum of three thousand dollars

with which to uniform and equip a boys'
temperance brigade which had been formed
in one of the ward churches a few months
before his campaign. Is it strange that the
good leader, whose heart was filled with innocent pride as he looked upon these promising young scions of virtue, should decline
to enter into a reform campaign? Of what
use to suggest that uniforms and bayonets
for the purpose of promoting temperance,
bought with money contributed by a man
who was proprietor of a saloon and a gambling house, might perhaps confuse the
ethics of the young soldiers? Why take
the pains to urge that it was vain to lecture
and march abstract virtues into them, so
long as the "champion boodler" of the town
was the man whom the boys recognized as
a loyal and kindhearted friend, the public-
spirited citizen, whom their fathers enthu-
siastically voted for, and their mothers called
"the friend of the poor." As long as the
actual and tangible success is thus embodied,
marching whether in kindergartens or bri-

gades, talking whether in clubs or classes,
does little to change the code of ethics.

The question of where does the money
come from which is spent so successfully,
does of course occur to many minds. The
more primitive people accept the truth-
ful statement of its sources without any
shock to their moral sense. To their simple minds he gets it "from the rich" and,
so long as he again gives it out to the poor
as a true Robin Hood, with open hand, they
have no objections to offer. Their ethics
are quite honestly those of the merry-mak-
ing foresters. The next less primitive people of the vicinage are quite willing to admit
that he leads the "gang" in the city council,
and sells out the city franchises; that he
makes deals with the franchise-seeking companies; that he guarantees to steer dubious
measures through the council, for which he
demands liberal pay; that he is, in short, a
successful "boodler." When, however, there
is intellect enough to get this point of view,
there is also enough to make the contention

that this is universally done, that all the aldermen do it more or less successfully, but
that the alderman of this particular ward is
unique in being so generous; that such a
state of affairs is to be deplored, of course;
but that that is the way business is run,
and we are fortunate when a kind-hearted
man who is close to the people gets a
large share of the spoils; that he serves
franchised companies who employ men in
the building and construction of their enterprises, and that they are bound in return
to give work to his constituents. It is
again the justification of stealing from the
rich to give to the poor. Even when they
are intelligent enough to complete the circle,
and to see that the money comes, not from
the pockets of the companies' agents, but
from the street-car fares of people like themselves, it almost seems as if they would
rather pay two cents more each time they
ride than to give up the consciousness that
they have a big, warm-hearted friend at court
who will stand by them in an emergency.

The sense of just dealing comes apparently much later than the desire for protection and indulgence. On the whole, the gifts and favors are taken quite simply as an evidence of genuine loving-kindness. The alderman is really elected because he is a good friend and neighbor. He is corrupt, of course, but he is not elected because he is corrupt, but rather in spite of it. His standard suits his constituents. He exemplifies and exaggerates the popular type of a good man. He has attained what his constituents secretly long for.

At one end of the ward there is a street of good houses, familiarly called "Con Row." The term is perhaps quite unjustly used, but it is nevertheless universally applied, because many of these houses are occupied by professional office holders. This row is supposed to form a happy hunting-ground of the successful politician, where he can live in prosperity, and still maintain his vote and influence in the ward. It would be difficult to justly estimate the influence which this group of successful, prominent men, including the alderman who lives there, have had upon the ideals of the youth in the vicinity. The path which leads to riches and success, to civic prominence and honor, is the path of political corruption. We might compare this to the path laid out by Benjamin Franklin, who also secured all of these things, but told young men that they could be obtained only by strenuous effort and frugal living, by the cultivation of the mind, and the holding fast to righteousness; or, again, we might compare it to the ideals which were held up to the American youth fifty years ago, lower, to be sure, than the revolutionary ideal, but still fine and aspiring toward honorable dealing and careful living. They were told that the career of the self-made man was open to every American boy, if he worked hard and saved his money, improved his mind, and followed a steady ambition. The writer remembers that when she was ten years old, the village schoolmaster told his little flock, without any mitigating clauses, that Jay Gould had laid the foundation of his colossal fortune by always saving bits of string, and that, as a result, every child in the village assiduously collected party-colored balls of twine. A bright Chicago boy might well draw the inference that the path of the corrupt politician not only leads to civic honors, but to the glories of benevolence and philanthropy. This lowering of standards, this setting of an ideal, is perhaps the worst of the situation, for, as we said in the first chapter, we determine ideals by our daily actions and decisions not only for ourselves, but largely for each other.

We are all involved in this political corruption, and as members of the community stand indicted. This is the penalty of a democracy, — that we are bound to move forward or retrograde together. None of us can stand aside; our feet are mired in the same soil, and our lungs breathe the same air.

That the alderman has much to do with setting the standard of life and desirable prosperity may be illustrated by the following incident: During one of the campaigns a clever cartoonist drew a poster representing the successful alderman in portraiture drinking champagne at a table loaded with pretentious dishes and surrounded by other revellers. In contradistinction was his opponent, a bricklayer, who sat upon a half-finished wall, eating a meagre dinner from a workingman's dinner-pail, and the passer-by was asked which type of representative he preferred, the presumption being that at least in a workingman's district the bricklayer would come out ahead. To the chagrin of the reformers, however, it was gradually discovered that, in the popular mind, a man who laid bricks and wore overalls was not nearly so desirable for an alderman as the man who drank champagne and wore a diamond in his shirt front. The district wished its representative " to stand up with the best of them," and certainly some of the constituents would have been ashamed to have been represented by a bricklayer. It is part of that general desire to appear well, the optimistic and thoroughly American belief, that even if a man is working with his hands to-day, he and his children will quite likely be in a better position in the swift coming to-morrow, and there is no need of being too closely associated with common working people. There is an honest absence of class consciousness, and a naïve belief that the kind of occupation quite largely determines social position. This is doubtless exaggerated in a neighborhood of foreign people by the fact that as each nationality becomes more adapted to American conditions, the scale of its occupation rises. Fifty years ago in America "a Dutchman" was used as a term of reproach, meaning a man whose language was not understood, and who performed menial tasks, digging sewers and building railroad embankments. Later the Irish did

the same work in the community, but as
quickly as possible handed it on to the Italians, to whom the name "dago" is said
to cling as a result of the digging which
the Irishman resigned to him. The Italian himself is at last waking up to this
fact. In a political speech recently made
by an Italian padrone, he bitterly reproached
the alderman for giving the-four-dollars-a-
day "jobs" of sitting in an office to Irish-
men and the-dollar-and-a-half-a-day "jobs" of
sweeping the streets to the Italians. This
general struggle to rise in life, to be at
least politically represented by one of the
best, as to occupation and social status, has
also its negative side. We must remember
that the imitative impulse plays an important part in life, and that the loss of social
estimation, keenly felt by all of us, is perhaps
most dreaded by the humblest, among whom
freedom of individual conduct, the power
to give only just weight to the opinion
of neighbors, is but feebly developed. A
form of constraint, gentle, but powerful,

is afforded by the simple desire to do
what others do, in order to share with
them the approval of the community. Of
course, the larger the number of people
among whom an habitual mode of conduct
obtains, the greater the constraint it puts
upon the individual will. Thus it is that
the political corruption of the city presses
most heavily where it can be least resisted,
and is most likely to be imitated.

According to the same law, the positive
evils of corrupt government are bound to
fall heaviest upon the poorest and least
capable. When the water of Chicago is
foul, the prosperous buy water bottled at
distant springs; the poor have no alternative but the typhoid fever which comes
from using the city's supply. When the
garbage contracts are not enforced, the
well-to-do pay for private service; the poor
suffer the discomfort and illness which are
inevitable from a foul atmosphere. The
prosperous business man has a certain
choice as to whether he will treat with

the "boss" politician or preserve his independence on a smaller income; but to an
Italian day laborer it is a choice between
obeying the commands of a political "boss"
or practical starvation. Again, a more intelligent man may philosophize a little
upon the present state of corruption, and
reflect that it is but a phase of our commercialism, from which we are bound to
emerge; at any rate, he may give himself
the solace of literature and ideals in other
directions, but the more ignorant man who
lives only in the narrow present has no
such resource; slowly the conviction enters
his mind that politics is a matter of favors
and positions, that self-government means
pleasing the "boss" and standing in with the
"gang." This slowly acquired knowledge he
hands on to his family. During the month
of February his boy may come home from
school with rather incoherent tales about
Washington and Lincoln, and the father
may for the moment be fired to tell of
Garibaldi, but such talk is only periodic,

and the long year round the fortunes of the entire family, down to the opportunity to earn food and shelter, depend upon the " boss."

In a certain measure also, the opportunities for pleasure and recreation depend upon him. To use a former illustration, if a man happens to have a taste for gambling, if the slot machine affords him diversion, he goes to those houses which are protected by political influence. If he and his friends like to drop into a saloon after midnight, or even want to hear a little music while they drink together early in the evening, he is breaking the law when he indulges in either of them, and can only be exempt from arrest or fine because the great political machine is friendly to him and expects his allegiance in return.

During the campaign, when it was found hard to secure enough local speakers of the moral tone which was desired, orators were imported from other parts of the town, from the so-called "better element."

Suddenly it was rumored on all sides that, while the money and speakers for the reform candidate were coming from the swells, the money which was backing the corrupt alderman also came from a swell source; that the president of a street-car combination, for whom he performed constant offices in the city council, was ready to back him to the extent of fifty thousand dollars; that this president, too, was a good man, and sat in high places; that he had recently given a large sum of money to an educational institution and was therefore as philanthropic, not to say good and upright, as any man in town; that the corrupt alderman had the sanction of the highest authorities, and that the lecturers who were talking against corruption, and the selling and buying of franchises, were only the cranks, and not the solid business men who had developed and built up Chicago.

All parts of the community are bound together in ethical development. If the so-called more enlightened members accept

corporate gifts from the man who buys up
the council, and the so-called less enlightened members accept individual gifts from
the man who sells out the council, we surely
must take our punishment together. There
is the difference, of course, that in the first
case we act collectively, and in the second
case individually; but is the punishment
which follows the first any lighter or less far-
reaching in its consequences than the more
obvious one which follows the second?

Have our morals been so captured by
commercialism, to use Mr. Chapman's gener-
alization, that we do not see a moral derelic-
tion when business or educational interests
are served thereby, although we are still
shocked when the saloon interest is thus
served?

The street-car company which declares that
it is impossible to do business without managing the city council, is on exactly the
same moral level with the man who cannot
retain political power unless he has a saloon,
a large acquaintance with the semi-criminal

class, and questionable money with which to
debauch his constituents. Both sets of men
assume that the only appeal possible is
along the line of self-interest. They frankly
acknowledge money getting as their own
motive power, and they believe in the cupid-
ity of all the men whom they encounter.
No attempt in either case is made to put
forward the claims of the public, or to find
a moral basis for action. As the corrupt
politician assumes that public morality is
impossible, so many business men become
convinced that to pay tribute to the corrupt
aldermen is on the whole cheaper than to
have taxes too high; that it is better to pay
exorbitant rates for franchises, than to be
made unwilling partners in transportation
experiments. Such men come to regard
political reformers as a sort of monomaniac,
who are not reasonable enough to see the
necessity of the present arrangement which
has slowly been evolved and developed, and
upon which business is safely conducted.

A reformer who really knew the people

DEMOCRACY AND SOCIAL ETHICS

and their great human needs, who believed
that it was the business of government to
serve them, and who further recognized the
educative power of a sense of responsibility, would possess a clew by which he might
analyze the situation. He would find out
what needs, which the alderman supplies,
are legitimate ones which the city itself
could undertake, in counter-distinction to
those which pander to the lower instincts of
the constituency. A mother who eats her
Christmas turkey in a reverent spirit of
thankfulness to the alderman who gave it to
her, might be gradually brought to a genuine
sense of appreciation and gratitude to the
city which supplies her little children with
a Kindergarten, or, to the Board of Health
which properly placarded a case of scarlet-
fever next door and spared her sleepless
nights and wearing anxiety, as well as the
money paid with such difficulty to the doctor and the druggist. The man who in his
emotional gratitude almost kneels before his
political friend who gets his boy out of jail,

might be made to see the kindness and good sense of the city authorities who provided the boy with a playground and reading room, where he might spend his hours of idleness and restlessness, and through which his temptations to petty crime might be averted. A man who is grateful to the alderman who sees that his gambling and racing are not interfered with, might learn to feel loyal and responsible to the city which supplied him with a gymnasium and swimming tank where manly and well-conducted sports are possible. The voter who is eager to serve the alderman at all times, because the tenure of his job is dependent upon aldermanic favor, might find great relief and pleasure in working for the city in which his place was secured by a well-administered civil service law.

After all, what the corrupt alderman demands from his followers and largely depends upon is a sense of loyalty, a standing-by the man who is good to you, who understands you, and who gets you out of trouble. All the social life of the voter from the time he was a little boy and played "craps" with his "own push," and not with some other "push," has been founded on this sense of loyalty and of standing in with his friends. Now that he is a man, he likes the sense of being inside a political organization, of being trusted with political gossip, of belonging to a set of fellows who understand things, and whose interests are being cared for by a strong friend in the city council itself. All this is perfectly legitimate, and all in the line of the development of a strong civic loyalty, if it were merely socialized and enlarged. Such a voter has already proceeded in the forward direction in so far as he has lost the sense of isolation, and has abandoned the conviction that city government does not touch his individual affairs. Even Mill claims that the social feelings of man, his desire to be at unity with his fellow-creatures, are the natural basis for morality, and he defines a man of high moral culture as one who thinks of himself, not as an isolated individual, but as a part in a social organism.

Upon this foundation it ought not to be difficult to build a structure of civic virtue. It is only necessary to make it clear to the voter that his individual needs are common needs, that is, public needs, and that they can only be legitimately supplied for him when they are supplied for all. If we believe that the individual struggle for life may widen into a struggle for the lives of all, surely the demand of an individual for decency and comfort, for a chance to work and obtain the fulness of life may be widened until it gradually embraces all the members of the community, and rises into a sense of the common weal.

In order, however, to give him a sense of conviction that his individual needs must be merged into the needs of the many, and are only important as they are thus merged, the appeal cannot be made along the line of self-interest. The de-

mand should be universalized; in this process it would also become clarified, and the
basis of our political organization become
perforce social and ethical.

Would it be dangerous to conclude that
the corrupt politician himself, because he
is democratic in method, is on a more
ethical line of social development than the
reformer, who believes that the people must
be made over by "good citizens" and gov-
erned by "experts"? The former at least
are engaged in that great moral effort of
getting the mass to express itself, and of
adding this mass energy and wisdom to
the community as a whole.

The wide divergence of experience makes
it difficult for the good citizen to understand this point of view, and many things
conspire to make it hard for him to act upon
it. He is more or less a victim to that curious feeling so often possessed by the good
man, that the righteous do not need to be
agreeable, that their goodness alone is sufficient, and that they can leave the arts and

wiles of securing popular favor to the self-
seeking. This results in a certain repellent
manner, commonly regarded as the apparel
of righteousness, and is further responsible
for the fatal mistake of making the surroundings of "good influences" singularly
unattractive; a mistake which really deserves a reprimand quite as severe as the
equally reprehensible deed of making the
surroundings of "evil influences" so be-
guiling. Both are akin to that state of
mind which narrows the entrance into a
wider morality to the eye of a needle, and
accounts for the fact that new moral movements have ever and again been inaugurated by those who have found themselves
in revolt against the conventionalized good.

The success of the reforming politician
who insists upon mere purity of administration and upon the control and sup-
pression of the unruly elements in the
community, may be the easy result of a
narrowing and selfish process. For the
painful condition of endeavoring to minister

to genuine social needs, through the political machinery, and at the same time to remodel that machinery so that it shall be adequate to its new task, is to encounter the inevitable discomfort of a transition into a new type of democratic relation. The perplexing experiences of the actual administration, however, have a genuine value of their own. The economist who treats the individual cases as mere data, and the social reformer who labors to make such cases impossible, solely because of the appeal to his reason, may have to share these perplexities before they feel themselves within the grasp of a principle of growth, working outward from within; before they can gain the exhilaration and uplift which comes when the individual sympathy and intelligence is caught into the forward intuitive movement of the mass. This general movement is not without its intellectual aspects, but it has to be transferred from the region of perception to that of emotion before it is really apprehended. The mass of men seldom move together without an emotional incentive. The man who chooses to stand aside, avoids much of the perplexity, but at the same time he loses contact with a great source of vitality.

Perhaps the last and greatest difficulty in the paths of those who are attempting to define and attain a social morality, is that which arises from the fact that they cannot adequately test the value of their efforts, cannot indeed be sure of their motives until their efforts are reduced to action and are presented in some workable form of social conduct or control. For action is indeed the sole medium of expression for ethics. We continually forget that the sphere of morals is the sphere of action, that speculation in regard to morality is but observation and must remain in the sphere of intellectual comment, that a situation does not really become moral until we are confronted with the question of what shall be done in a concrete case, and are obliged to act upon our theory. A stirring appeal has lately been made by a recognized ethical lecturer who has declared that "It is insanity to expect to receive the data of wisdom by looking on. We arrive at moral knowledge only by tentative and observant practice. We learn how to apply the new insight by having attempted to apply the old and having found it to fail."

This necessity of reducing the experiment to action throws out of the undertaking all timid and irresolute persons, more than that, all those who shrink before the need of striving forward shoulder to shoulder with the cruder men, whose sole virtue may be social effort, and even that not untainted by self-seeking, who are indeed pushing forward social morality, but who are doing it irrationally and emotionally, and often at the expense of the well-settled standards of morality.

The power to distinguish between the genuine effort and the adventitious mistakes is perhaps the most difficult test which comes to our fallible intelligence. In the

range of individual morals, we have learned
to distrust him who would reach spirituality
by simply renouncing the world, or by
merely speculating upon its evils. The
result, as well as the process of virtues
attained by repression, has become distasteful to us. When the entire moral energy
of an individual goes into the cultivation
of personal integrity, we all know how
unlovely the result may become; the character is upright, of course, but too coated
over with the result of its own endeavor to
be attractive. In this effort toward a higher
morality in our social relations, we must
demand that the individual shall be willing
to lose the sense of personal achievement,
and shall be content to realize his activity
only in connection with the activity of the
many.

The cry of " Back to the people " is always heard at the same time, when we have
the prophet's demand for repentance or
the religious cry of " Back to Christ," as
though we would seek refuge with our fel-

lows and believe in our common experiences as a preparation for a new moral struggle.

As the acceptance of democracy brings a certain life-giving power, so it has its own sanctions and comforts. Perhaps the most obvious one is the curious sense which comes to us from time to time, that we belong to the whole, that a certain basic well being can never be taken away from us whatever the turn of fortune. Tolstoy has portrayed the experience in "Master and Man." The former saves his servant from freezing, by protecting him with the heat of his body, and his dying hours are filled with an ineffable sense of healing and well-being. Such experiences, of which we have all had glimpses, anticipate in our relation to the living that peace of mind which envelopes us when we meditate upon the great multitude of the dead. It is akin to the assurance that the dead understand, because they have entered into the Great Experience, and therefore must comprehend all lesser ones; that all the misunderstandings we have in life are due to partial experience, and all life's fretting comes of our limited intelligence; when the last and Great Experience comes, it is, perforce, attended by mercy and forgiveness. Consciously to accept Democracy and its manifold experiences is to anticipate that peace and freedom.

INDEX[1]

Alderman, basis of his political success, 226, 228, 240, 243, 248, 267; his influence on morals of the American boy, 251, 255, 256; on standard of life, 257; his power, 232, 233, 235, 246, 260; his social duties, 234, 236, 243, 250.

Art and the workingman, 219, 225.

"Boss," the, ignorant man's dependence on, 260, 266.

Business college, the, 197.

Charity, administration of, 14, 22; neighborly relations in, 29, 230; organized, 25; standards in, 15, 27, 32, 38, 49, 58; scientific vs. human relations in, 64.

Child labor, premature work, 41, 188; first laws concerning, 167, 170.

City, responsibilities of, 266.

Civil service law, its enforcement, 231, 233.

Commercial and industrial life, social position of, compared, 193.

Commercialism and education, 190–199, 216; morals captured by, 264; polytechnic schools taken by, 202.

Coöperation, 153, 158.

Cooper, Peter, 202.

Dayton, Ohio, factory at, 216.

Death and burials among simple people, 238.

Domestic service, problem of, in France, England, and America, 135; industrial difficulty of, 106; moral issues of, 106.

Education, attempts at industrial, 201; commercialism in, 196, 201; in commercialism, 216; in technical schools, 201; lack of adaptation in, 199, 208, 212; of industrial workers, 180, 193, 199, 219; offset to overspecialization, 211; public school and, 190, 192; relation of, to the child, 180, 185, 193; relation of, to the immigrant, 181–186; university extension lectures and settlements, 199; workingmen's lecture courses, 214.

Educators, mistakes of, 212; new demands on, 178, 192, 201, 211.

Family claim, the, 4, 74, 78; daughter's college education, 82; employer's vs. domestic's, 123, 124; on the daughter, 82; on the son, ibid.

Family life, misconception of, 116.

Filial relations, clash of moral codes, 94.

Funerals, attitude of simple people toward, 238.

Household employee, the, 108, 109; character of, 112; domestic vs.

---

[1] This index is not intended to be exhaustive.

INDEX

INDEX

Workingman, the, ambition of, for his children, 191, 258; art in relation to, 218; charity of, 154; evening classes and social entertainment for, 189; grievance of, 211; historical perspective in the work of, *ibid.;* organizations of, 214; standards for political candidate, 257.

THE JOHN HARVARD LIBRARY